EDUCATION IN SCOTLAND

Education in Scotland is markedly different from that in the rest of the United Kingdom – with a different curriculum, school boards to oversee school management and a General Teaching Council which has been in existence since 1965.

Whilst there are many examples of successful and innovative practice in Scotland, the system is quite often not recognised as different by writers who talk about the United Kingdom education system as if it were one smooth whole. This book describes recent developments in both legislation and practice in Scotland, drawing comparisons with the English system. Chapters cover administration and management, early years education provision, the curriculum in Scotland, secondary education and special educational needs.

Margaret Clark is Emeritus Professor of Education at the University of Birmingham. **Pamela Munn** is Professor of Curriculum Research at Moray House Institute of Education, Edinburgh.

EDUCATION IN SCOTLAND

Policy and practice from pre-school to secondary

Edited by Margaret M. Clark and Pamela Munn

London and New York

First published 1997
by Routledge
11 New Fetter Lane, London EC4P 4EE

Simultaneously published in the USA and Canada
by Routledge
29 West 35th Street, New York, NY 10001

Typeset in Palatino by
BC Typesetting, Bristol
Printed and bound in Great Britain by
Creative Print and Design (Wales), Ebbw Vale

British Library Cataloguing in Publication Data
A catalogue record for this book is available from the British Library

Library of Congress Cataloguing in Publication Data
Education in Scotland: policy and practice from pre-school to
secondary/edited by Margaret M. Clark and Pamela Munn.
    p.   cm.
Includes index.
ISBN 0–415–15835–4 (hardcover: alk. paper). –
ISBN 0–415–15836–2 (pbk.)
    1. Education–Scotland–Evaluation.   2. Education and state-
-Scotland.   3. School management and organization–Scotland.
I. Clark, Margaret MacDonald.   II. Munn, Pamela.
LA652.E25   1997
370'.9411–dc21   97-14247
                                                                    CIP

CONTENTS

List of contributors   vii
Preface   xi
Acknowledgements   xiii
Abbreviations   xiv

1 EDUCATION IN SCOTLAND: SETTING THE SCENE
   Margaret M. Clark   1

2 THE UNDER-FIVES: FROM 'PRE-SCHOOL
   EDUCATION' TO 'EARLY YEARS SERVICES'
   Joyce Watt   19

3 DEVELOPMENTS IN PRIMARY EDUCATION
   IN SCOTLAND
   Margaret M. Clark   35

4 THE STATUTORY YEARS OF SECONDARY
   EDUCATION: CHANGE AND PROGRESS
   Brian Boyd   52

5 UPPER-SECONDARY EDUCATION
   David Raffe   67

6 SPECIAL EDUCATIONAL PROVISION
   Alison Closs   81

7 THE TEACHING PROFESSION:
   ITS QUALIFICATIONS AND STATUS
   Margaret M. Clark   98

8 STANDARDS AND QUALITY
   Pamela Munn   115

v

CONTENTS

9   DEVOLVED MANAGEMENT OF SCHOOLS
    Pamela Munn   125

10 POLICY-MAKING IN SCOTTISH EDUCATION:
    A CASE OF PRAGMATIC NATIONALISM
    Lindsay Paterson   138

11 HOW SCOTTISH IS THE SCOTTISH CURRICULUM:
    AND DOES IT MATTER?
    Cameron Harrison   156

12 FUTURE DIRECTIONS?
    Pamela Munn   170

    Useful Addresses   181
    Index   183

CONTRIBUTORS

EDITORS

Margaret M. Clark is Emeritus Professor of Education at the University of Birmingham. She was educated in Scotland and has taught at primary school, college of education and universities in Scotland. After her move to England in 1979 as Professor of Education at the University of Birmingham she kept in touch with developments in Scotland, for several years as Assessor in Education for the University of Strathclyde. She has undertaken research into many aspects of education, funded by the Scottish Education Department and the Department of Education and Science, and was personally commissioned by the Secretary of State for Education to undertake an evaluation of research of relevance to the education of children under five. In 1988 she was awarded the Scottish Council for Research in Education's Fellowship for her distinguished contribution to educational research. Her publications include the internationally quoted *Young Fluent Readers* (Heinemann, 1976) and *Children Under Five: Educational Research and Evidence* (Gordon and Breach, 1988).

Pamela Munn is Professor of Curriculum Research at Moray House Institute of Education, Edinburgh. Her previous posts include those of Depute Director of the Scottish Council for Research in Education and a lectureship at the University of York. She is a researcher of over fifteen years' standing, attracting substantial funds from a range of research bodies and charities. She has published widely on school discipline and on school governance. She was awarded the SCRE silver medal for the most promising young researcher in 1982. Her most recent books are

Parents and Schools: Customers, Managers or Partners? (Routledge, 1993) and (as co-author) two companion volumes on school discipline: *Effective Discipline in Secondary Schools and Classrooms* and *Effective Discipline in Primary Schools and Classrooms* (Paul Chapman, 1992). She sits on the editorial boards of a number of national and international journals.

CONTRIBUTORS

Brian Boyd is Associate Director of Quality in Education at the University of Strathclyde. He has taught in a junior secondary school, been headteacher of a comprehensive school and was Chief Adviser in Strathclyde Region. He has written extensively on Scottish education and is currently involved in school improvement research.

Margaret M. Clark is Emeritus Professor of Education at the University of Birmingham. She was educated in Scotland and has taught at primary school, college of education and universities in Scotland. She has undertaken research into many aspects of education, funded by the Scottish Education Department and the Department of Education and Science.

Alison Closs is Lecturer in Special Needs/Support for Learning, Moray House Institute of Education, Edinburgh. Her interests in teacher education and research include the links between disadvantage, cultural differences, difficulties in learning and teacher attitudes. Current research concerns the education of children with serious medical conditions, and Romany and refugee children.

Cameron Harrison is the Chief Executive of the Scottish Consultative Council on the Curriculum, a post he has held since 1991. The Council is the principal advisory body on the school curriculum for 3–18-year-olds. He is associated with a number of academic institutes within Scotland and has written extensively on the curriculum and on managing change within education systems.

Pamela Munn is Professor of Curriculum Research at Moray House Institute of Education, Edinburgh. Her previous posts include those of Depute Director of the Scottish Council for Research in Education and a lectureship at the University of York. She is a researcher of over fifteen years' standing, attracting substantial funds from a range of research bodies and charities. She has published widely on school discipline and on school governance.

Lindsay Paterson is Professor of Educational Policy at Moray House Institute of Education, Edinburgh. He has worked at the Centre for Educational Sociology at the University of Edinburgh and has published on many aspects of the sociology of education – in particular on the effects of social disadvantage and on the expansion of higher education, and on Scottish politics and culture. His most recent books are *Politics and Society in Scotland*, with Alice Brown and David McCrone (Macmillan, 1996) and *The Autonomy of Modern Scotland* (EUP, 1994). He is vice-convenor of the Unit for the Study of Government in Scotland, and edits its quarterly journal, *Scottish Affairs*.

David Raffe is Professor of Sociology of Education at the University of Edinburgh. He directs the Centre for Educational Sociology and co-directs the Institute for the Study of Education and Society. His research interests include secondary and post-secondary education and the labour market, with particular emphasis on the post-compulsory education and training systems of Scotland and other countries.

Joyce Watt is Reader in Education at the University of Aberdeen. She has wide experience of early education and of educational disadvantage in Scotland as a primary teacher, lecturer in teacher education and researcher. She has published widely and has contributed to national and international conferences in both fields for many years.

PREFACE

People use the term 'British education' when what they really mean is English education. The Scots have a long and proud tradition of a distinctive education system. This book describes the key features of Scottish education and highlights the main differences from the English system. It is a must for those interested in the different ways in which schools are organised, the curriculum is arranged and teachers are trained. It is especially pertinent at a time when many countries are reviewing their curricula and standards.

The book covers the stages of education in Scotland from pre-school to secondary. It contains chapters written by acknowledged experts in their fields. It reviews provision at pre-five, the 5–14 programme, Scotland's rather different version of a national curriculum, the 14–16 curriculum and the distinctive approach taken to upper-secondary education called Higher Still. It raises questions about how Scottish the curriculum is and speculates about whether such distinctions as there are will continue. There are also chapters on special education and on the education of teachers, with particular reference to the role and function of the General Teaching Council. The book considers the policy context in which education operates and discusses the devolved management of schools, Scottish style, as well as the scope for a separate education policy.

This is the first major book for over twenty years giving a comprehensive overview of Scottish education. It will help readers answer the question of whether education in Scotland really is superior to that elsewhere in the United Kingdom and, if it is, suggest the possible reasons for this. This book is a must for anyone interested in standards and quality and in attempts to ensure parity of esteem between vocational and academic courses, and for students of public policy.

ACKNOWLEDGEMENTS

The editors wish to express their thanks to all the many colleagues and friends who have read and commented on the proposal for the book and drafts of the various chapters. We are also grateful to all those individuals and departments in central and local government who have supplied us with information. We hope they will understand that we are no less grateful for not mentioning them by name. We are particularly grateful to Lesley Scullion, who coped with successive drafts and last-minute alterations efficiently and with good humour.

ABBREVIATIONS

COSLA	Convention of Scottish Local Authorities
CRDU	Children's Rights Development Unit
CSE	Certificate in Secondary Education
CSYS	Certificate of Sixth Form Studies
DES	Department of Education and Science
DfEE	Department for Education and Employment
EIS	Educational Institute of Scotland
GTC	General Teaching Council for Scotland
HMI	Her Majesty's Inspectorate
NCVQ	National Council for Vocational Qualifications
OFSTED	Office for Standards in Education
QNCA	Qualifications and National Curriculum Authority (replaces SCAA and NCVQ)
SCAA	School Curriculum and Assessment Authority
SCCC	Scottish Consultative Council on the Curriculum
SCE	Scottish Certificate of Education
SCET	Scottish Council for Educational Technology
SCOTVEC	Scottish Vocational Education Council
SCRE	Scottish Council for Research in Education
SEB	Scottish Examination Board
SED	Scottish Education Department
SHEFC	Scottish Higher Education Funding Council
SOED	Scottish Office Education Department
SOEID	Scottish Office Education and Industry Department
SPPA	Scottish Pre-School Playgroups Association
SPTC	Scottish Parent Teacher Council
SQA	Scottish Qualifications Authority (replaces SEB and SCOTVEC)

SRC	Strathclyde Regional Council
SSBA	Scottish School Board Association
TVEI	Technical and Vocational Education Initiative

1

EDUCATION IN SCOTLAND
Setting the scene
Margaret M. Clark

In recent years there have been major changes in education in the United Kingdom, in the curriculum and in the assessment of achievement, in management and inspection of schools and in the education of teachers. The impression is often given that developments in Scotland differ little from those elsewhere in the United Kingdom; that is an erroneous impression which this book should dispel. The book is aimed at a wide readership overseas as well as in the United Kingdom. As will be seen, many of the issues being confronted in Scotland today, and the proposed solutions, have relevance to educationists in many countries.

This chapter provides readers with a brief outline of education in Scotland. Where the organisation and developments differ fundamentally from those in England, this is indicated in italics. Brief reference is made to issues considered in the following chapters; there full reference lists are to be found. Where developments are relevant to more than one chapter, the context is set out here.

SCOTLAND: THE BACKGROUND TO EDUCATION

In 1997, Scotland, with a population of about 5 million, is part of the United Kingdom (which also includes England, Wales and Northern Ireland), with a total population of about 58 million. The political structures in the United Kingdom in the twentieth century may be a puzzle to readers from other countries – particularly the claim that there is a distinctive system of governing Scotland, since there has been no separate legislature in modern times. The

1

United Kingdom Parliament is in London, and only a minority of Members of Parliament from Scotland belonged to the government which was in power for eighteen years to 1997 (at the General Election in 1992 only 11 of 72 seats in Scotland were won by Conservatives, and at the General Election in 1997 there were no Conservative MPs returned from Scotland). Yet, even under a Conservative government that has been described as hostile to Scottish distinctiveness many distinctive features survived, particularly with regard to education and the legal system. There have, however, been increasing strains since the late 1970s (see Brown, McCrone and Paterson 1996). Lindsay Paterson discusses policy-making in Scottish education in Chapter 10. The 'Scottishness' of the curriculum in Scotland is considered by Cameron Harrison in Chapter 11.

Although for some aspects there are separate Acts of Parliament for Scotland, they must be passed by the Parliament in Westminster. Prior to the General Election which took place in May 1997, there was debate as to whether and to what extent Scottish affairs should become independent of England. With the advent of a Labour government, this debate is now heightened. Autonomy could entail complete state independence, probably inside the European Union, thus putting Scotland in a position analogous to that of Denmark and Sweden; or it could involve the devolution of some legislative powers and responsibilities from Westminster to a directly elected Scottish Parliament. Whatever the outcome, the issues discussed in this book will still be pertinent, and the distinctiveness of Scottish education is likely to remain. In Chapter 12 Pamela Munn considers this and other issues concerning the future of Scottish education.

Two important background features are of relevance to education in Scotland. First, Scotland is the most sparsely populated part of the United Kingdom, and second, there are high levels of poverty in some areas. In 1995 about 20 per cent of the school population were entitled to free school meals; this varied from about 6 per cent in the Borders Region to about 40 per cent in the City of Glasgow. In Glasgow in 1993, one in three children lived in households dependent on income support and one in two of all primary-school children received clothing grants. The focus for many of the early interventions into educational disadvantage was the densely populated urban areas, which is not surprising when one considers the level of deprivation in some urban areas. However, since the early 1990s a range of national research and development projects have been initiated in rural areas. In many cases these have been linked with economic regeneration (Nisbet and Watt 1993).

THE ADMINISTRATION OF EDUCATION IN SCOTLAND

Education in Scotland has been organised separately from that in England and Wales since the Union of 1707, and there are separate Acts of Parliament governing most aspects of Scottish education. The school system was initially developed by the churches and formally came under the Scotch (later Scottish) Education Department from 1872. For more than a decade after that, resources were directed towards the provision of an efficient system of elementary education; very few children went to secondary school. Between 1872 and 1885 one education department covered the whole of the United Kingdom. At that time, the governing bodies which had the greatest impact on schooling, however, were the HMI (which have always been based in Scotland) and the school boards (or their predecessors). In 1885, Parliament established an independent Scotch Education Department, initially in London. The Scottish Education Department (SED), subsequently based in Edinburgh, has been re-named several times, first as the Scottish Office Education Department (SOED); currently it is the Scottish Office Education and Industry Department (SOEID). The Scottish Office, which is in Edinburgh, has a ministerial team headed by the Secretary of State for Scotland, who is a member of the Cabinet. In the Scottish Office there is an Education and Industry Department headed by its own minister.

The Secretary of State for Education is the Cabinet minister responsible for education in England, and the relevant department is currently the Department for Education and Employment. Parallel changes in the name of the responsible department have taken place in England, with the Department of Education and Science (DES) changing to DfE and now DfEE.

Between 1975 and 1996 there were two tiers of local government in Scotland, Regions and districts, except for three island

3

all-purpose authorities. Education was the responsibility of the 9 Regions and 3 island authorities. Strathclyde Region both covered a very large and diverse area geographically and included about half the population. In 1996, 29 single-tier councils replaced the 9 former Regions and 53 districts. The 3 small all-purpose island councils (Orkney, Shetland and Western Isles) have remained in place. Some of the fears with regard to education which dominated the parliamentary passage of the legislation have not been realised, since all the councils have appointed directors of education and education committees although they were not statutorily obliged to do so. Some of the committees have other responsibilities, and one has subsumed education within a children's committee. More varied approaches and structures are likely to emerge with 32 smaller education authorities; it is too early to assess the impact of the change. However, virtually all councils have given high priority to pre-fives and special needs. Stress is also being placed on quality measures and on projects to improve literacy. The major problem for the new councils is the budgetary restrictions under which they are operating. (See TES Scotland 1996 for a leaflet setting out the details of the new councils, their education officials and a summary of their plans.)

The structure described above applied to most sections of Scottish education, with two exceptions, the universities which were answerable ultimately to government departments in London, and certain types of colleges run directly by the Scottish Education Department. These exceptions have now ended: all institutions of higher education have been directly overseen since 1993 by the Scottish Higher Education Funding Council, and the control of the vocational colleges of further education was transferred from local government to the Scottish Office.

SCOTTISH EDUCATION STATISTICS

The publication of official statistics on Scottish education dates back well over a hundred years. The information for this section has been taken from the most recent information on numbers of schools, teachers and pupils in the first of a new series of publications, *Scottish Education Statistics* (SOEID 1996). Similar documents are published for England, Wales and Northern

Ireland. As the statistics cover the years 1990–1 to 1994–5 the breakdown of information is in terms of the former education authorities.

Schools in Scotland fall into four main groups:

1 Education authority schools are financed partly by central government and partly by local taxation. These are under the management of local authorities, responsible for the allocation of funding. School boards, consisting of parents and teachers co-opted from the local community, with parents in the majority, have been established in about three-quarters of education authority schools.
2 Two schools (at June 1996) had self-governing status, that is, were funded direct from central government.
3 Independent schools are run by the proprietors without any aid from public funds. Some of these schools participate in the assisted places scheme which provides financial assistance for secondary pupils who would otherwise not be able to attend an independent school (these places the Labour government plans to phase out).
4 A small number of grant-aided schools, mainly in the special sector, are run by boards of managers who receive grants from central government.

Nursery schools provide education on a full-or part-time basis for children below compulsory school age. Children enter primary school at the beginning of the school year in August if they will be five years of age by the end of February of that school year. Primary schools have children aged from 5 to 12 years of age (P1 to P7); secondary schools are for pupils from 12 to 16–18 depending on when the individual pupils choose to leave school (S1 to S6).

Scotland has no equivalent of the Sixth Form College or Tertiary College.

The following is the information on schools/departments in Scotland in 1994–5, with the numbers of pupils in each type of school in brackets:

Schools/Departments		Pupils
Education authority schools		
Nursery	784	(49,760)
Primary	2,336	(438,010)
Secondary	405	(314,907)
Special*	318	(8,712)
Other		
Grant-aided schools†	9	(1,472)
Independent schools	116	(32,579)

* The figure for special schools in SOEID 1996 refers to both schools and departments based in schools outside the special sector. I understand that the information on special education will in future not be presented in that form as pupils who attend special departments are otherwise integrated into the school curriculum. As stated in Chapter 6, there were 201 special schools in 1994–5 (see that chapter for further information on special education).

† The majority of the grant-aided schools joined the independent sector in 1985.

The total school population in Scotland in 1994–5 was 845,440, of whom about 96 per cent were in local authority schools; most of the remaining 4 per cent attended independent schools.

In contrast, in England in 1996 according to DfEE 1 in 5 state secondary-school pupils was being educated in a grant-maintained school. There are 1,100 GM schools, primary, secondary and special. Since 1994 the Funding Agency for Schools has been responsible for the calculation and payment of grants to GM schools.

The numbers of (full-time equivalent) teachers in schools in Scotland were as follows in 1994–5:

Education authority schools	50,014
Grant-aided schools	162
Independent schools	3,207

Pupil–teacher ratios are given in the statistics for different types of school and for each education authority. It would not be helpful to quote these, however, as averages are particularly misleading in a country like Scotland where there are many small rural schools; indeed, in some education authorities most of the primary schools have fewer than 100 pupils on roll and many classes are composite classes. There are over one hundred primary schools with 20 pupils or under. In 1994 more than half the primary schools in Scotland had 200 pupils or fewer on roll, and 64 of 406 secondary schools had 400 or fewer on roll.

The size of the school roll is an important factor in the budgeting costs per pupil: in general, the smaller the school, the higher the cost per pupil. The national average cost for secondary-school pupils in Scotland remains significantly higher than that for primary pupils. In 1995–6 primary schools with rolls above 300 had budgeted running costs per pupil in the range £1,000-£2,000. Most secondary schools with rolls above 800 had budgeted running costs per pupil in the range £2,000-£3,000; however, a school with a roll of 300 might have budgeted running costs per pupil around 50 per cent higher than a school with a roll of 800 (see HMI 1996a).

No education statistics are available from the Scottish Office for pupils whose mother tongue is not English, or who are from ethnic minorities. It is clear from the available census figures, however, that the picture in Scotland is very different from that in England.

According to the 1991 census only 1.4 per cent of the population in Scotland over three years of age speak, read or write Gaelic. The largest concentrations are in the Western Isles, Highland and Strathclyde Regions. However, over the past ten years there has been support from the Scottish Office for the teaching of Gaelic and through the medium of Gaelic (see Chapter 3).

According to the 1991 census, Scotland's population was about five million, 98.7 per cent of whom were white. Thus only 1.3 per cent of the population were from ethnic minorities, of whom the vast majority were of Pakistani or Indian origin; the second largest group was Chinese. The majority of the non-white population are concentrated in Glasgow and Edinburgh.

In England in 1991 6.2 per cent of the population were from ethnic minorities.

THE UNDER-FIVES

While Scotland has its own policy-making procedures for the care and education of its under-fives, the organisational framework is similar to that of the rest of the United Kingdom, and like the rest of the country Scotland is one of the most poorly served parts of the European Union in terms of under-fives provision. The roots of early years education in Scotland lie in poverty and educational disadvantage.

Lack of funding has stemmed partly from the fact that services for under-fives have been outside the statutory education service and therefore frequently subjected to cuts. Furthermore, fragmentation of services has been a consequence of the fact that responsibility for pre-fives services has been divided at both national and local level, between education and social work departments. An exception was the former Strathclyde Region, which made a pioneering attempt to bring the services together under its education department. The recently established Stirling council has taken the radical step of establishing a children's committee which aims to integrate all services in pre-fives education with services in social work, play and family support. Indeed, committee structures and the management of early years services are now under active discussion by all the new unitary authorities, and new patterns are emerging. Thus, attempts are being made to increase the level of provision for pre-fives; to get rid of the false distinctions between 'education' and 'care'; to increase the partnership between the public, voluntary and private sectors; and to introduce quality assurance procedures as for other public-sector services.

In Scotland, as in England, the Conservative government introduced a pilot voucher scheme to enable parents of four-year-olds to purchase a part-time place in any approved under-fives group. It is unlikely that the proposed extension of this scheme, which has been highly controversial, will survive the recent change of government. Developments in the care and education of under-fives is discussed by Joyce Watt in Chapter 2.

THE CURRICULUM AND ASSESSMENT IN SCOTTISH SCHOOLS

There have been major developments in the curriculum and in assessment in Scotland, as in England and Wales, over the past ten years; however, the changes have increased rather than reduced the differences between education in Scotland and that in England and Wales.

The Scottish Consultative Council on the Curriculum (SCCC) is the principal advisory body to the Secretary of State for Scotland on all matters relating to the curriculum for 3–18-year-olds. It keeps the Scottish school curriculum under review; issues guidance on the curriculum to local authorities and to schools; and carries out programmes of curriculum development, consulting with interested groups and individuals. Its recent publication *Teaching for Effective Learning*, which was the subject of widespread consultation, has met with an enthusiastic response (SCCC 1996). SCCC has launched its largest ever consultation, including businesses, unions, cultural agencies, the churches, political parties and the media, on the place of Scottish culture in schools. It has extensive international links, and for the past three years has provided the Secretariat for CIDREE (Consortium of Institutions for Development and Research in Education in Europe); this will continue for a further three years.

There is not a national curriculum in Scotland. The national guidelines in the 5–14 Programme developed between 1987 and 1993 are based on the reports of working parties of professionals closely involved in work in the schools. Unlike the national curriculum in England and Wales, they do not represent a sharp change from previous policy. The guidelines lay emphasis on balance, breadth and continuity in children's learning. Thus they cover the seven years of primary education, and the first two years of secondary education. An outline of the programme is to be found in *The Structure and Balance of the Curriculum 5–14* (SOED 1993), and further details of its implications for primary education are to be found in Chapter 3.

The implementation of the guidelines for English and mathematics in primary schools is well under way. The target is for all the guidelines to be implemented by 1998–9. Assessment and reporting form an integral part of the programme, with emphasis on teacher assessment, and materials for diagnostic assessment in English, mathematics and science are already available. National tests in English and mathematics which were initially to have been administered in P4 and P7 are now seen as a support for teacher assessment, administered at the teachers' discretion, not at specific points in a child's schooling. The tests are prepared by the 5–14 Assessment Unit in the Scottish Examination Board, which issues a catalogue from which teachers select tests. No league tables are prepared on the basis of the national tests; indeed, it would not be possible to do so in view of the way they are constructed and administered. The results are communicated only to the parents of the individual pupils.

Disappointment has been expressed at the limited influence of the guidelines on the first two years of secondary education, where mixed ability teaching predominates, and at standards in these years, including those revealed in the recently published international survey. Under discussion are the possibility of 'setting' in the early years of secondary schooling and proposals that there should be national testing during that stage of secondary education, which some feel would cut across the aims of the national guidelines for 5–14 with their emphasis on continuity from primary to secondary education. Neither the issue of 'setting' versus mixed ability teaching nor that of national testing in S1 or S2 has so far been resolved.

There was active promotion of comprehensive education in Scotland in the late 1960s and increasing numbers of pupils stayed on in school beyond the statutory leaving age, which in 1972 was raised to sixteen. There are no selective public (maintained) schools in Scotland. In the 1970s two parallel committees were established: the Dunning committee, which considered assessment in upper secondary school, and the Munn committee, which reviewed the structure of the curriculum in the third and fourth years of secondary school. In Chapter 4 Brian Boyd discusses curriculum and assessment for the age range 12–16.

In England, in contrast, new committees were established in the Education Reform Act 1988, which also laid down the framework for national testing, named 'Key Stages', and identified the Core and other Foundation Subjects in the national curriculum for 5–16. Subsequently changes have been made to the committee structure and aspects of the national curriculum. A particularly controversial issue has been the publication of league tables based on the results of national tests at the end of each Key Stage, the first when children are 7 years of age (for this there is no parallel in Scotland).

Post-fourteen-year-olds in Scotland take courses leading to awards in the Scottish Certificate of Education at Standard Grade and Higher Grade, and/or Scottish Vocational Education Council modules. They can also take the Certificate of Sixth Year Studies in the final year. Examinations for the Scottish Education Certificate have until now been the responsibility of the Scottish

Examination Board; the other examinations have been the responsibility of the Scottish Vocational Educational Council. The two bodies are now amalgamated under the newly established Scottish Qualification Authority (SQA). In 1988 the Scottish 'Higher' examination for school leavers was one hundred years old. In 1965 responsibility for the examinations was handed over to an examination board consisting of representatives of the Department, the teaching profession, the universities and other interested parties.

In 1990 the Secretary of State established a committee, the Howie committee, to review the aims and purposes of the courses and assessment in S5–S6. It had been felt that the Higher Grade syllabus was too academically orientated for the increasing numbers of pupils staying on at school beyond the statutory leaving age and that there was insufficient time between the Standard Grade examinations and the Higher Grade. Although some aspects of the Howie Report were favourably received, there was concern at the proposed twin-track courses. In 1994 the Scottish Office produced a less radical plan which it proposes to introduce in 1999. The reform, set out in *Higher Still: Opportunity for All* (Scottish Office 1994), will offer a wide range of courses, and pupils will be able to take a mix of vocational and academic subjects leading to qualifications which will have equal status and recognition. Higher Still is the first curricular development which has offered 'opportunity for all' from its inception by its creation of a special educational advisory group to guide developments and a team of development officers to work in all subject areas. Many young people with special educational needs now progress to college. Upper-secondary education for 15–18-year-olds is discussed by David Raffe in Chapter 5.

Although the primary purpose of the Scottish Examination Board has been to set examinations which reflect the school curriculum, the Board has played a formative role in curricular development and in new approaches to learning. There has been a close partnership between the Board and practising teachers. For further information see *A Short History of National School Certificates in Scotland* (Philip 1995).

In England there is also consideration of the relationship of academic to vocational courses in upper-secondary with the merger in 1997 of the School Curriculum and Assessment Authority (SCAA) and the National

Council for Vocational Qualifications to form the Qualifications and National Curriculum Authority. There are, however, major differences in qualifications awarded in upper-secondary education in England, one of which is earlier selection for A levels, with students taking a much narrower range of subjects. Unlike Scotland, in England schools choose from a number of examination boards, each with its own syllabus – and, it is suggested, possibly also with different standards.

SPECIAL EDUCATIONAL PROVISION

Special educational provision is subject to Scottish Office control and specifically Scottish legislation; however, much responsibility is devolved to local authorities. Pupils between the ages of 2 and 19 are included, with school attendance mandatory for the 5–16 age group. Local authorities are required to identify children and young persons who have pronounced, specific or complex educational needs which require continuing review, and to open and keep a Record of Needs for them. Appeals about recording and placement are addressed by the Sheriff Court or by HMIs acting on behalf of the Secretary of State for Scotland.

Special educational provision may take place in mainstream classes, units within ordinary schools, special schools and other locations. Currently 1.2 per cent of school pupils are educated in special schools, with little change over recent years. There are over 14,000 pupils with Records of Needs, of whom over a third spend all their time in mainstream classes. Curricular support for individual pupils in mainstream classes is generally provided by a learning support teacher working for short periods of time with the class or subject teacher; in some cases practical help is also given by an auxiliary.

The Record of Needs is equivalent to the Statement of Needs in England and Wales, where a special tribunal deals with appeals.

THE TEACHING PROFESSION: ITS ROLE AND STATUS (See Chapter 7)

The General Teaching Council

There has been a General Teaching Council (GTC) in Scotland for over thirty years. It is a statutory body, working closely with

SOEID, but independent of it. It is funded by the annual fees paid by registered teachers. In 1996 there were over 77,000 teachers on the register. It is illegal for an education authority to employ a teacher in a nursery, primary, special or secondary school who is not registered with the Council; most private schools also prefer to employ registered teachers. The Council plays a major role in Scottish education: It regulates entry to the profession; has a powerful voice in the vetting of initial training courses for teachers; and is responsible for the assessment of probationary teachers.

Teacher education

The minimum entry requirements to courses are determined by the Secretary of State for Scotland in consultation with GTC. For the teaching qualification in primary education, courses must be designed to teach children in the 3–12 age range. There are two alternative courses: a four-year Bachelor of Education degree and a Postgraduate Certificate of Education, which follows the award of a university degree. There are three routes to the teaching qualification in secondary education, which must prepare students to teach pupils in the age range 12–18 in one or more named subjects. These are a one-year PGCE following an appropriate degree; a four-year B.Ed. degree in some subjects; and a combined degree.

Assessment of quality of teacher education

During 1994–5 evaluations of all the courses leading to B.Ed., PGCE and combined degrees were undertaken, and the findings published. The quality of the teacher education in all institutions was judged as at least satisfactory, and in most, highly satisfactory.

The professional development of teachers

There have recently been major developments with the establishment of a common framework in Scotland for credit-based learning. During the 1990s, most colleges of education have either become part of universities or have developed closer links, making institutional collaboration easier. The three-tier structure, with flexible modular schemes and credit transfer, provides teachers with the possibility of planning their programme to meet their needs and is an encouragement to continuing professional development.

In England the Teacher Training Agency is the body responsible for overseeing the training of teachers, and there is so far in 1997 no General Teaching Council.

STANDARDS AND QUALITY

There are several major sources of evidence; these are considered in Chapter 8 by Pamela Munn. Two important sources are noted here.

The first is HM Inspectorate's programme of independent inspection. HMIs in Scotland have been appointed by Royal Warrant since 1840. Within the Inspectorate there is an Audit Unit which was established in 1992. The Unit, which is concerned with issues such as the relationship between money spent, or resources bought, and the quality of education achieved, has an extensive list of publications, including information on examination results, school costs, leavers' destinations, attendance, truancy and performance, and a series of publications on school development planning (available from SOEID). The results of inspections are analysed centrally by the Audit Unit, making use of performance indicators completed by individual inspectors and inspection teams. *Standards and Quality in Scottish Schools 1992–95* (HMI 1996b) gives an account of how well schools are performing in the seven key areas in HMI performance indicators.

A 'quality culture' initiative has resulted in publication, after piloting, of performance indicators which are used in inspection. Schools are themselves encouraged to use these for their self-evaluation and in forming development plans (see McGlynn and Stalker 1995). A Scottish Schools Ethos Network has recently been established, jointly sponsored by HM Audit Unit and Moray House Institute of Education, to which individual schools, education authorities and organisations can belong. This is to support schools engaged in self-evaluation of their ethos through sharing of expertise and experience.

A second source of evidence about standards is the Assessment of Achievement Programme, established in 1981, directed by the Research and Intelligence Unit in SOEID. This involves surveys of performance on samples of pupils throughout Scotland in mathematics, English language and science. Concern has been expressed recently at the proposal that SOEID might no longer commission independent researchers to undertake the surveys.

OFSTED (the Office for Standards in Education), established in 1992, is responsible for inspection of schools in England, but has no jurisdiction in Scotland. In England, since the closing of the Assessment of Performance Unit, there have not been regular surveys of attainment in the main curricular areas which enable national comparisons over time to be made in levels of performance.

DEVOLVED MANAGEMENT OF SCHOOLS
(See Chapter 9)

Parental choice and involvement in schools have been an important aspect of developments in educational policy in recent years in the United Kingdom. Three main aspects of policy are distinctively different from the situation in England. Parental choice legislation, which was introduced in Scotland in 1981, gave stronger rights of choice of school. School boards, which were not established until 1988, have more limited powers than those of governing bodies in England and Wales, in the area of school finance, for example. There are important differences in the ways in which budgetary control is devolved from the local authority to schools; one difference is that in Scotland it is devolved directly to the headteacher, not to the school board. Introduced later than in England, this aspect will not be fully operational until 1998. Government pronouncements about the aims and purposes of boards stress three main functions: the greater involvement of parents in school affairs, closer community involvement and freeing education authorities progressively from the business of routine school administration.

In England and Wales extensive powers are now devolved to governing bodies.

EDUCATIONAL RESEARCH

Scotland has a long and distinguished record of educational research, much of it involving practising teachers, local authorities and colleges as well as university education departments. It is not

15

possible to give details of the extensive network of educational research which is currently underway or the major national and international studies. The contributors to this book, who are active researchers, make reference to a number of important studies in the following chapters. Here two centres from which further information on policy-related research can be obtained are noted.

The Research and Intelligence Unit in SOEID is responsible for planning a wide range of research in education; providing research-based advice for ministers and others; disseminating research; and encouraging and maintaining interest and expertise in educational research in schools, colleges, universities and research institutes.

The Scottish Council for Research in Education, founded in 1928, conducts research and disseminates research findings – including research done by other institutions. It is also the home-base for the Scottish Teacher-Researcher Support Network, which assists teachers to carry out their own research studies. It is funded by contracts from organisations which include government departments, local authorities, charitable foundations and international bodies. It has a major contract with SOEID which covers a range of activities.

The equivalent body in England is the National Foundation for Educational Research.

LEARNING TO SUCCEED IN SCOTLAND

A Commission on Scottish Education was set up in 1994 following the publication of the report of the National Commission on Education, *Learning to Succeed*, which had a United Kingdom-wide remit and whose comments on Scottish education were generally favourable (National Commission on Education 1993). The Scottish Commission had a limited remit: to consider the gaps in the report, in Scottish terms. The focus is on those issues in Scottish education and training which require strategic decisions over the medium and long term (Commission on Scottish Education 1996).

The Commission considered Scotland better placed than other parts of the United Kingdom to achieve a number of the goals it set. Among the advantages it sets out on p. 14 are:

- greater public confidence in the changing education system
- a General Teaching Council to help ensure quality in teaching
- a greater link between academic and vocational qualifications
- the existence of a Scottish Assessment of Achievement Programme
- national testing confined to language and mathematics
- the development of 'ethos indicators' by the Scottish Inspectorate.

The gaps it perceived include the following:

- the early years
- school effectiveness
- courses and qualifications for 16–18-year-olds
- further education, training and community education
- higher education
- governance and accountability.

In the following chapters the strengths and weaknesses of aspects of Scottish education will be considered. Higher and further education, training and community education are not covered.

REFERENCES

Brown, A., McCrone, D. and Paterson, L. (1996) *Politics and Society in Scotland*, Basingstoke: Macmillan.

Commission on Scottish Education (1996) *Learning to Succeed in Scotland: A Radical Look at Education Today and a Strategy for the Future*, Edinburgh: The Commission on Scottish Education.

HMI (1996a) *Scottish Schools: Costs 1993/94 to 1995/96*, Edinburgh: Audit Unit, SOEID.

—— (1996b) *Standards and Quality in Scottish Schools 1992–95*, Edinburgh: Audit Unit, SOEID.

McGlynn, A. and Stalker, H. (1995) 'Recent developments in the Scottish process of school inspection', *Cambridge Journal of Education* 25(1): 13–21.

National Commission on Education (1993) *Learning to Succeed: A Radical Look at Education Today and a Strategy for the Future*, London: Heinemann.

Nisbet, J. and Watt, J. (1993) *Educational Disadvantage in Scotland: A 1990s Perspective*, Edinburgh: Scottish Community Education Council.

Philip, H. (1995) *A Short History of National School Certificates in Scotland*, Dalkeith, Midlothian: Scottish Examination Board.

SCCC (1996) *Teaching for Effective Learning*, Dundee: SCCC.

Scottish Office (1994) *Higher Still: Opportunity for All*, Edinburgh: HMSO.

SOED (1993) *The Structure and Balance of the Curriculum 5–14*, Edinburgh: HMSO.

SOEID (1996) *Scottish Education Statistics: 1996 Edition No. 1*, Edinburgh: Government Statistical Service, SOEID.

TES Scotland (1996) *The Essential Guide to the 32 Education Authorities: Councils '96*, leaflet included on 29 March.

2

THE UNDER-FIVES
From 'pre-school education' to 'early years services'

Joyce Watt

While Scotland has its own policy-making procedures for the care and education of its under-fives, it shares its organisational framework with the rest of the United Kingdom. The terminology is similar: 'nursery schools and classes', 'day centres', 'family centres', 'pre-school playgroups', 'private nurseries', 'community nurseries' and 'childminding' have largely common meanings. Like other parts of the United Kingdom, Scotland has no national policy for its under-fives: provision is non-statutory and therefore variable, often reflecting its origins in social welfare policies for disadvantaged areas.

In contrast to England, across Scotland there are no differences in entrance policies to primary schools. In Scotland, admission is only once a year, in August, for those with birthdays between 1 March that year and the last day of February the following year. This leaves a large number of 'under-fives' in primary schools, although fewer than south of the Border. This is one of the many reasons why there has long been an assumption that the care and education of children under five should be coordinated with provision for children in the first two or three years of the primary school as services for 'the early years'. 'Under-five', then, is a stage in its own right, but it is also part of 'the early years': one of its problems is that it often finds it difficult to be both.

Changes in terminology are not accidental. 'Under-fives' is itself a relatively recent term. It reflects the principle of including even the youngest babies and establishes the identity of the whole age group as a distinctive stage. The term 'pre-school' is used much less than previously since it implies a function defined by schooling. The most recent generic term is 'early years services'. The vision is of a range of services for all children from birth to eight over-riding departmental as well as sectoral boundaries and recognising that each stage is interdependent but significant in its own right. It is an 'inclusive' model which puts services based on the needs of young children at the heart of a national welfare system for families.

Changes in terminology reflect wider changes in thinking about the role and function of under-fives services. In Scotland, as in the rest of the United Kingdom, the service struggles to reconcile the best of its past with current demands for change: it is trying hard to rid itself of false distinctions between the 'education' and 'care' of young children still reflected in national as well as many local authority structures; and it is rethinking the relationship between the public, voluntary and private sectors. It is also trying to come to terms with its dual function as a service for children based also on the needs of families and communities and its more narrowly educational function as provider of the first stage in promoting children's academic achievement, a duality reflected in the terms 'early years services' and 'pre-school education'. Finally, it is establishing formal quality assurance procedures in all its under-fives provision as for other public services.

Despite sharing this background with the rest of the United Kingdom, Scotland's under-fives services have their own distinctive cultural roots, and they take a deep pride in their distinctive identity. National legislative and policy documents for local authorities are issued through the Scottish Office and carry their own Scottish stamp. National organisations also have their own distinctive identity. The Scottish Pre-school Playgroups' Association and the Scottish Childminders' Association, for example, operate in parallel but separately from their counterparts south of the Border and Children in Scotland works in close partnership with the National Children's Bureau and Children in Wales but retains its status as an independent agency.

This chapter, then, examines contemporary trends in under-fives provision in the context of specifically Scottish policy and practice and highlights some of the issues which are arising as 'pre-school education' and 'early years services' move forward together. Five policy issues are highlighted: provision, coordination, children's rights, the voucher system and the curriculum. The chapter ends with a discussion of what might be meant by 'inclusion' in 'early years services' in Scotland in the closing years of the century.

PROVISION OF SERVICES

Any discussion of provision for under-fives in Scotland must acknowledge two factors referred to in the Introduction to this volume, poverty and rural isolation. Scotland's levels of relative poverty are notoriously high, and much traditional under-fives provision has been a response from local authorities and the voluntary sector to resulting problems of educational and social disadvantage. The need and the response remain to the present day. Long, Macdonald and Scott (1996) claim that 42 per cent of children under five in Scotland are still living in relative poverty, and Tennant (1995) highlights the particular problems of single mothers with children under five unable to find employment because of the lack of affordable child care. Local authorities and voluntary organisations alike have given a high priority to children in poverty through their admission policies and through a huge range of innovative projects. Most have common aims: to highlight the impact of poverty on families with young children, to provide a range of services for both children and adults in cooperation with the families themselves, and to work in partnership with other similarly committed providers.

Despite the fact that Scotland has by far the lowest population density in the United Kingdom, that rural poverty is widespread, and that economic activity rates for women with dependent children are high, the issue of how to provide quality child care and education for young children in rural areas has had, until recently, a very low national profile (although the pre-school playgroup movement has long been active in rural Scotland). Since the early 1990s, however, a range of national research and development projects have been initiated, and local authorities with rural constituencies, including those which are predominantly urban in nature, have begun to invest in their rural hinterlands. A particular feature of many rural developments in child care has been their links with economic regeneration. Nevertheless, in both urban and rural areas, provision remains fragmented and inadequate.

In terms of more general levels of provision, Scotland shares with the rest of the United Kingdom the unenviable reputation of being one of the most poorly served parts of the European Union (Moss 1996). Although levels of provision in Scotland may be improving, less than 2 per cent of under-fives are accommodated in local authority day centres and family centres (Children in Scotland 1995), and in 1994 (the last year for which figures are available) only 38 per cent of 3- and 4-year-olds had a place (almost all part-time) in a local authority nursery school or class (Scottish Office 1995a). Provision was also very uneven across the country. For example, while most of the mainly urban local authorities provided a nursery school or class place for around 50 per cent of their 3- and 4-year-old children, others provided much less and one rural authority provided none at all. A further problem is that very little publicly funded provision suits the mother in employment because most is part-time. In Scotland, women now constitute around half of the total workforce. For the majority of those with young children, child care becomes a major issue: many use a range of individual informal family and neighbourhood arrangements, but most are forced into the private sector. The dramatic rise in the number of registered childminders in Scotland (Scottish Office 1995a) is one reflection of the demand.

Like other parts of the United Kingdom, then, Scotland in 1997 has a fragmented range of services where demand far exceeds supply, particularly for public provision, where a parent's chance of obtaining a place in the kind of service and with the hours and facilities she wants depends mostly on luck, on where the family happen to live and on the ability to pay. Until a national policy is agreed and implemented, the problems of fragmentation and the impossibility of matching need with supply will remain.

COORDINATION OF SERVICES

At the heart of this fragmentation lies the historical anomaly that responsibility for under-fives services is divided at both national and local authority levels between education and social work departments, the former responsible for 'education' in nursery schools and classes and the latter for the traditional 'care' services as well as for the registration and review of playgroups, private groups and childminders. Given the conceptual alignment of these two functions in present-day thinking, it is bureaucratic nonsense that this situation continues.

The exception to the general rule was the former Strathclyde Region, which, more than a decade ago, and with considerable vision, brought all its under-fives services together under the aegis of its education department (Stratchclyde Regional Council 1985).

The aim was to provide, as part of the region's 'social strategy', a universal service for under-fives and their families free of charge. That could only be done through an integrated service. It was a move which at the time brought a new status and importance to the under-fives field in what was by far the largest local authority in Scotland, but it also generated intense political and professional controversy (Penn 1992) and, in retrospect, is seen by many to have been visionary but unrealistic.

It was a move which, at the time, was unique in the United Kingdom, although several English authorities have now followed a similar course. It remained unique among the Scottish Regions until the reorganisation of local government and the demise of Strathclyde as a local authority in March 1996, when the integrated under-fives service was inherited by some of the new unitary authorities in the south-west of Scotland. Committee structures and the management of early years services are now under active discussion by all new unitary authorities and new patterns are emerging. Stirling council, for example, has taken the radical step of establishing a children's committee which aims to integrate all services in pre-five education with services in social work, play and family support.

CHILDREN'S RIGHTS TO QUALITY SERVICES

Children's rights have become an issue in Scotland as elsewhere since the late 1980s, and the rights of young children to quality care and education are now formally recognised. The United Kingdom as a whole was a signatory to the United Nations Convention on the Rights of the Child (1989), but, because Scotland's legal system and many of its policies relating to children and young people were different, Scotland had its own unit, the Scottish Children's Rights Development Unit (CRDU), to implement the Convention's principles through a specifically 'Scottish Agenda'. Among its conclusions relating to young children was that both central and local government policies in Scotland denied many children and families the right to child care under Articles 18.2 and 3 of the United Nations Convention (Children's Rights Development Unit 1994: 13).

The Children Act 1989 and the Children (Scotland) Act 1995 pursue the rights of young children in terms of quality provision. The Children Act 1989 relates mainly to England and Wales, but

Part X (Sections 1–79) and Part III (Section 19) also relate to the regulation and review of childminding, day care and education services for children under eight in Scotland. The Act made it mandatory on local authorities to set up quality assurance procedures for all under-fives services registered with their social work departments (local authority nursery schools and classes were already monitored through inspections from Her Majesty's Inspectors (HMIs). The Act also required local authorities to bring together their education and social work departments in consultation with health boards, voluntary organisations, employers and parents to review and report on services for under-eights every three years. These reviews were completed in 1992 and 1995.

The wider issues of child care for Scotland are included in the Children (Scotland) Act 1995, which, like the 1989 Act, is based on the principles of children's rights, cooperation among welfare agencies and partnership with parents. Of most relevance to the present discussion are the new duty on local authorities, under Section 27, to provide day care for 'children in need' and, under Section 19, to prepare, consult upon and publish plans for children's services including early years services. Since the 1995 Act became law from November 1996, there has been extensive debate about the nature and definition of 'children in need', how the legislation will affect provision for under-fives, and how the new unitary authorities will be able to plan for 'children's services'.

VOUCHERS

The Conservative government's proposals for a nursery 'voucher' scheme for children in their pre-school year in Scotland have now been incorporated into the Education (Scotland) Act 1996 and parallel legislation in England and Wales. Under the scheme, parents of eligible children receive a 'voucher' to the value of £1,100 which can be exchanged for a part-time place in any approved under-fives group. Education authority nursery schools and classes, as well as classes within independent schools, are automatically approved, while private and voluntary groups must be registered under the Children Act 1989 and must satisfy HMI of their quality. The pilot schemes have operated in four areas of Scotland (North Ayrshire, East Renfrewshire, parts of Argyll & Bute and parts of Highland) since late 1996, and are being evaluated by a research team at Stirling University. It was intended that the scheme would be implemented nationally by 1997. However, the Labour government which is now in power is committed to abolishing the scheme.

As in England, the scheme has been highly controversial. Responses to the Scottish Office's consultation paper on the future of pre-school education in Scotland (Scottish Office 1995b) were largely negative (Long 1996). Objections were wide-ranging:

- that the consultation process itself was confined to the implementation of the scheme and ignored the principles involved;
- that the scheme, which was ostensibly about parental choice, ignored the acknowledged fact that what parents wanted was more local authority nursery provision;
- that it was consumer led;
- that it threatened provision for younger children;
- that there was no guarantee of more places and for some children the voucher would therefore be worthless;
- that the value of the voucher itself was too low;
- that the scheme would lead to greater inequalities;
- that quality of provision would be endangered;
- that the administrative costs were high and the work was being inappropriately assigned to a private agency; and
- that the whole scheme, because it was based on competition between providers, would put in jeopardy the long painstaking process of collaboration which had been built up over the years.

In short, both the voluntary and public sectors were firmly opposed to the proposals (Long 1996: 35). Despite this reaction, the Scottish Office, in December 1995, invited local authorities to bid for a place on the pilot scheme. Six applied and four were selected.

The nursery voucher scheme has now become a political issue throughout the United Kingdom, with the Labour Party which is now in power committed to its demise. Not surprisingly, the Scottish scheme had a frosty reception from opposition parties when it was debated at the Scottish Grand Committee in Stirling in January 1996. All expressed serious reservations: most were scathing. However, while providers are clearly unhappy, the scheme has been put firmly in the hands of the consumers, the parents. We await the parents' judgement.

THE CURRICULUM

The most recent general statement from the Scottish Office on the under-fives curriculum (SOED 1994) was based largely on HMI visits to a range of under-five units. It reiterated the importance of play and emphasised the importance of cultivating children's 'natural learning processes' through a carefully planned 'curriculum' in every kind of under-fives unit, not just nursery schools and classes. It even extended the notion of the 'curriculum' to what parents do with their children at home and emphasised the importance of coordinating the curriculum of the home with that of the under-fives group. The report was, however, largely a restatement of accepted principles and made little attempt to relate the under-fives play-based curriculum to the increasingly structured 'areas of knowledge' approach embodied in the various National Curriculum Guidelines for 5–14 issued by SOED from 1993 which children would meet on their entry into primary school.

That question had, however, already been tackled in some local authorities. Lothian Region, for example, had produced its own guidelines, *A Curriculum for the Early Years* (Lothian Regional Council 1992), which included the first years of the primary school. The document states clearly the local authority's commitment to the wider aims of early years education.

> The aim of early education is to help young children to think, become confident, aware, creative and caring, with the ability to communicate and to relate to their environment and the people in it.
>
> (p. 3)

At the same time, the document begins to tackle constructively how the 5–14 Programme could be used to further these wider aims both at the under-fives level and in the first years of the primary school. Strathclyde Region too linked its curriculum guidelines for under-fives to the 5–14 Programme (Strathclyde Regional Council 1994). The overall message is still one of a 'learning partnership' between child and adult and the process is still firmly embedded in play, but informal links with the primary curriculum are spelt out. All local authority curriculum documents of the 1990s, however, differ from those produced a decade previously in their new emphasis on planning and evaluation.

This new emphasis on planning, self-evaluation and 'quality' is also reflected in the Scottish Office's publication of performance indicators for self-evaluation in under-fives groups (SOED 1995). The emphasis is on 'audit', on determining the strengths and weaknesses of the unit as it is, and finding starting points for improvement. It is to be a continuous process firmly in the hands of the unit's own management team and staff in consultation with parents.

The most recent document from the Scottish Office is its consultation draft on the curriculum for children in the year before they enter primary school (SOEID 1996). This document is clearly linked to the voucher scheme. Play is still seen to be central since 'it makes a powerful contribution to children's development and learning' (p. 5), but this time the purpose of the pre-school year as preparation for the primary school is more evident. The link with the 5–14 Programme is clear, particularly in the emphasis on 'outcomes of learning',

> [which] emphasise literacy and numeracy as well as emotional, personal, creative and physical skills and contribute to children's knowledge and understanding of the world.
>
> (p. 4)

There is also a narrowness of purpose. The 'vital contribution' which 'pre-school education' is said to make is in leaving children confident, eager and enthusiastic learners who are looking forward to starting school (p. 3). Nevertheless, this Scottish document is more liberal and less prescriptive than its counterpart south of the Border (SCAA 1996). The expected 'outcomes' are less rigid and the educational process of linking the under-fives curriculum with the curriculum of the primary school is left largely where it belongs, with those who will be responsible for its implementation.

'INCLUSION' AND EARLY YEARS SERVICES

'Inclusion' contrasts with the term 'exclusion', which is used by the European Commission to describe the condition of those who, because of social factors, are unable to grasp life's opportunities in ways open to their more fortunate peers. Many under-fives groups in Scotland were founded to combat 'exclusion' and to promote the 'inclusion' of all children in that sense. Today, 'early years services' still have that aim, but the task is viewed much more broadly and is seen as a corporate responsibility. 'Inclusion' is also therefore a useful concept both to examine how the notion of 'early years services' tries to promote a more corporate identity for what is offered to young children and to highlight some of the gaps and discontinuities of present provision. It is important to note in passing that aspects of the 'inclusion' debate are highly controversial, but discussion of them is beyond the scope of this chapter.

Inclusion in under-fives groups

One of the obvious trends towards 'inclusion' of recent years has been to extend all services more genuinely to the whole under-fives age range, not simply the 3–5 age group. Indeed, there is now an emphasis in some parts of the voluntary sector on the birth to three age group partly because these are the most critical years of all for human development and partly because, as provision generally has improved for older groups, the voluntary sector has been able to concentrate its resources more on the youngest children.

As we have also noted, there is still in Scotland a huge emphasis on encouraging and supporting vulnerable groups – disadvantaged urban and rural families, ethnic minorities and disabled children – within the wider aim of universal provision. It is clear, however, that a universal system of under-fives services free at the point of need is totally unrealistic in the short term, and priorities will therefore continue to operate. But who decides what the priorities should be? Central government? Local authorities? Communities? Individual units? Part of the resentment towards the voucher scheme has been that in providing a universal service for all children in their pre-school year, central government has been seen to have put traditional priorities in jeopardy and to have provided a universal service for one age group at the expense of vulnerable families and younger children.

Under-fives provision is also increasingly 'inclusive' in the way it tries to meet the educational and care needs not only of young children but of their families and, in some cases, through them the needs of the community as a whole. Adult education and vocational training, counselling services, health services, welfare rights groups, drop-in services and after-school care are now common features of many under-fives units, particularly family centres. Most recently, the 'community nursery', the 'flagship of Strathclyde's integrated pre-five policy', has set out to provide a fully inclusive service under one roof (Wilkinson, Kelly and Stephen 1993).

The community nursery probably exemplifies best another issue of inclusion which has beset the under-fives sector over many years, how to provide common training and qualifications for under-fives workers. This is not the place to discuss such a major issue. Suffice it to say here that, despite recent national developments such as Scottish Vocational Qualifications and changes in both teacher and nursery nurse training (Holman and Kleinberg 1994), this is a field still rife with problems. Inclusive frameworks of training are now, however, under active discussion.

There are also interesting issues of 'inclusion' to be explored in relation to the under-fives curriculum. For example, in the not too distant past it would have been unlikely for any part of the under-fives sector other than nursery schools and classes to consider that they were operating a 'curriculum' at all and, even in the nursery sector, there might have been some reservation about the apparent formality of the word. Most early years workers did take very seriously the kind of activities they offered children, but 'curriculum' was something associated with schools and professional teaching. Now, as we have seen (SOED 1994), all early years workers are responsible for the implementation of a 'curriculum' and the concept has even been extended to the home. No longer, then, is the under-fives curriculum the prerogative of professional teachers in nursery schools. More than that, as the recent consultation draft from the Scottish Office makes clear (SOEID 1996), all groups from the public, private and voluntary sectors which are registered for the voucher scheme will be expected to operate within broadly the same curriculum framework.

That same paper in its outline of the learning opportunities and outcomes which should be part of the pre-school curriculum emphasises that this is a curriculum to which all children are *entitled* (my italic). This is a relatively new concept for under-fives, but it implies principles of inclusion where all children will be guaranteed as far as possible the tools for making the most of life's chances. It also echoes recent thinking within the debate on educational standards in primary schools, particularly those in disadvantaged areas. Schemes of 'early intervention' in the form of focused programmes in the early years of the primary school are increasingly seen as critical for children in disadvantaged areas if they are to achieve the standards of literacy and numeracy to which they are 'entitled'. Lothian Region's Early Intervention in Reading programme, which has been running since the early 1990s, and Dundee's READ project (Raising Standards of Educational Achievement in Dundee) are good examples. One striking feature of these and other intervention programmes is the increasing involvement of the school psychological service and the re-emergence of formal testing in the early years of the primary school. The inevitable corollary of this trend is that we are now beginning to see the widespread development of screening programmes as children move from their under-fives groups into the primary school.

Inclusion and the primary-school curriculum

If pre-school education is to be effective, it must have strong links with the curriculum of the primary school. As we have already noted, there was widespread recognition that the 5–14 Programme should bring in its wake some reassessment of the under-fives curriculum, although it was also accepted that the under-fives curriculum should not simply be a preparation for the primary school. This principle was largely maintained in the recent consultation document on 'the curriculum for the pre-school year' (SOEID 1996). Nevertheless, the development of the 5–14 Programme has generated a lot of uncertainty among staff in under-fives units, particularly nursery schools and classes. In a recent study of ninety-six (mostly four-year-old) children in a variety of under-fives settings, Powney et al. (1995) found that two-thirds of the time was spent in activities directly related to the 5–14 Programme. Malcolm and Byrne (1996), however, found that some primary teachers did not want to know what children had achieved in 5–14 terms. Some, indeed, wanted to know only whether children had reached particular landmarks such as knowing their colours. Teachers could discover the rest for themselves. Powney *et al.* (1995) conclude that staff in under-fives units are left very uncertain about what is expected of them.

While there may be all kinds of practical problems relating to curriculum continuity and the keeping of useful records, the most deeply rooted problem is that, whatever the previous experience and learning of children entering primary school, primary teachers want to think of children making a 'fresh start'. This is a difficulty at every transitional change. Harlen (1996) in her overview of the first four years of the 5–14 Programme comments:

> in terms of continuity in progress for the individual pupil, the entrenched preference for a 'fresh start' and lack of interest in records and work sent by pupils' previous teachers remain a cause for some concern.
>
> (p. 31)

At the transition to the primary school this is particularly disturbing since not all children entering the primary school will come with the skills and understanding necessary to tackle the first stages of the 5–14 Programme.

Powney *et al.* (1995) also found that, of 300 under-fives centres studied, only 17 reported liaison on the curriculum with the primary school and that, while some form of liaison existed between most local authority under-fives groups and their primary school, fewer than half of playgroups and private groups had any links. This, coupled with the fact that most liaison was one-way and that primary staff rarely visited pre-five settings, leaves us in no doubt on whose terms the inclusion of the under-fives curriculum in the transition process depends. If the implementation of the link between the under-fives curriculum and the curriculum of the primary school is to be left in the hands of practitioners rather than policy-makers, as we have suggested it should be, this lack of liaison is a cause for concern.

Inclusion and parents

Finally, those who have been increasingly 'included' in under-fives groups in the past few decades are parents. Even if the practice varies widely (sometimes justifiably), we are now well beyond the stage of having to make a case for the inclusion of parents in their child's education. A wider discussion of the role of parents in Scottish education is found in Chapter 9, but three points are worth highlighting in the context of the under-fives. First, there can be no genuine 'early years services' without parents, since the education of young children is the education of young families. Second, many under-fives groups, particularly in disadvantaged areas, are the first step for many mothers in the process of 'empowerment', whereby individuals, groups and communities learn to take responsibility for their own development and a pride in the ownership of their own lives.

Third, parents must be included in the under-fives curriculum. In the wake of the publication of the national curriculum guidelines 5–14, Macbeth and Watt (1994) claimed that the rhetoric of a 'partnership' with parents in the primary school was largely meaningless and confined to very small and very occasional gestures on the school's terms (p. 16). The recent consultation paper from the Scottish Office on the curriculum in the pre-school year (SOEID 1996) is little better. Here again the rhetoric is about a 'partnership' akin to that implied in the 5–14 guidelines. Teachers should

> recognise the contribution of parents to their children's learning and suggest ways that they can support their learning at home.
>
> (p. 37)

Again the assumption is that the direction of influence is one-way. This is not to deny the importance of helping parents of young children to extend their 'school' learning at home. Nor is it to deny that the model of partnership which both these curriculum documents espouse is probably taken for granted by many Scottish parents. Macbeth (1994), for example, argues:

> The belief that a school can provide a total education is deeply engrained in Scottish thinking.
>
> (p. 7)

Fortunately, however, many under-fives groups have moved with their parents beyond this traditional stance.

Finally, while educational provision for under-fives in Scotland remains non-statutory and large sectors of it remain outside the official province of local authority education departments, it cannot be said to be a fully inclusive part of the Scottish educational system. It does, however, share with that system a deep pride in its distinctive Scottish identity and a desire for ownership of its own future. Current trends towards the development of 'early years services' and pressure for a national policy for under-fives can succeed only if they acknowledge that as their starting point.

REFERENCES

Children in Scotland (1995) *Scotland's Families To-day*, Edinburgh: Children in Scotland.

Children's Rights Development Unit (1994) *Scottish Agenda for Children*, Glasgow: CRDU.

Harlen, W. (1996) *Four Years of Change in Education 5–14*, Edinburgh: Scottish Council for Research in Education.

Holman, A. and Kleinberg, S. (1994) 'Training for Quality in Early Education', in J. Watt (ed.) *Early Education: The Quality Debate*, Edinburgh: Scottish Academic Press.

Long, G. (1996) *A Report on Responses to 'The Future of Scottish Pre-School Education'*, Glasgow: Scottish Early Years and Family Network, Glasgow Caledonian University.

Long, G., Macdonald, S. and Scott, G. (1996) *Child and Family Poverty in Scotland: The Facts*, 2nd edn, Glasgow: Glasgow Caledonian University and Save the Children (Scotland).

Lothian Regional Council (1992) *A Curriculum for the Early Years*, Edinburgh: Lothian Regional Council.

Macbeth, A. (1994) 'Why parents matter in education', in *Parents and the 5–14 Curriculum*, Dundee: Scottish Consultative Council on the Curriculum.

Macbeth, A. and Watt, J. (1994) 'Parents and the curriculum: aspects of theory and practice', in *Parents and the 5–14 Curriculum*, Dundee: Scottish Consultative Council on the Curriculum.

Malcolm, H. and Byrne, M. (1996) *5–14 in the Primary School: The First Four Years*, Edinburgh: Scottish Council for Research in Education.

Moss, P. (1996) 'Perspectives from Europe', in G. Pugh (ed.) *Contemporary Issues in the Early Years: Working Collaboratively for Children*, London: Paul Chapman.

Penn, H. (1992) *Under Fives: The View from Strathclyde*, Professional Issues in Education Series No. 8, Edinburgh: Scottish Academic Press.

Powney, J., Glissov, P., Hall, S. and Harlen, W. (1995) *We are Getting them Ready for Life: Provision for Pre-fives in Scotland*, Edinburgh: Scottish Council for Research in Education.

SCAA (1996) *Nursery Education: Desirable Outcomes for Children' Learning*, London: DfEE.

Scottish Office (1995a) *Provision for Pre-school Children*, Statistical Bulletin, Education Series, Edn/A2/1995/16, June 1995.

— (1995b) *The Future of Scottish Pre-school Education*, Consultation Paper, Edinburgh: The Scottish Office, July 1995.

SOED (1993) Curriculum and Assessment in Scotland: National Guidelines, *The Structure and Balance of the Curriculum 5–14*, Edinburgh: HMSO.

—— (1994) *The Education of Children Under 5 in Scotland*, Edinburgh: HMSO.

—— (1995) *Using Performance Indicators in Nursery School/Class/Pre-Five Unit Self Evaluation*, Edinburgh: HMSO.

SOEID (1996) *A Curriculum Framework for Children in their Pre-school Year*, A Consultative Draft by Her Majesty's Inspectors of Schools, Edinburgh: HMSO.

Strathclyde Regional Council (1985) *Under Fives*, Glasgow: SRC.

—— (1994) *Partners in Learning*, Glasgow: SRC.

Tennant, R. (1995) *Children and Family Poverty in Scotland: The Facts*, 1st edn, Glasgow: Glasgow Caledonian University and Save the Children (Scotland).

Wilkinson, J.E., Kelly, B. and Stephen, C. (1993) *Flagships: An Evaluation Research Study of Community Nurseries in Strathclyde 1989–1992*, Glasgow: Department of Education, University of Glasgow.

3

DEVELOPMENTS IN PRIMARY EDUCATION IN SCOTLAND

Margaret M. Clark

INTRODUCTION

In Scotland, as in England and Wales, there have been major developments in the curriculum and in assessment in primary schools over the past ten years. The 5–14 Development Programme which was initiated in Scotland over the period 1987–93 has taken the form of a series of national guidelines, based on reports of working parties of professionals closely involved in work in the schools. The recent changes in Scotland, in contrast to England, do not represent a sharp change from previous policy. The 5–14 Programme is intended to give clarification and guidance, with a stress on balance, breadth and continuity in children's learning over the ages 5–14. The aim of the national guidelines and recommendations for assessment is to provide teachers, parents, pupils and others with a clearer statement of what schools can reasonably expect children to attain between the ages of 5 and 14. In Scotland, as in England, there was a 'child-centred report' in the 1960s, *Primary Education in Scotland* (SED 1965). There does not appear to have been a backlash against the report, which is often referred to as the 'Primary Memorandum', as there has been recently in England against the Plowden Report (DES 1967). Indeed, the developments in Scotland reflect many of the views expressed in the Primary Memorandum on the purpose and nature of primary education.

In this chapter a brief reminder will be given of the organisation of education in Scotland in so far as it is relevant to understanding primary education (see Chapter 1 for further information). The extent to which recent developments mirror the recommendations of the Primary Memorandum of 1965 will be considered. The national guidelines 5–14 and related assessment documents will then be discussed as far as they apply to primary schools and their links with secondary schools. Where appropriate a comparison will be made with the changes in primary education in England since 1988. Evidence of the extent to which the national guidelines appear so far to be influencing practice in primary schools in Scotland will be considered. Brief reference will be made to recent projects involving modern languages and Gaelic-medium units in primary schools.

THE STRUCTURE OF PRIMARY EDUCATION IN SCOTLAND

The following are key features:

1 Teachers in primary schools in Scotland must be registered with the General Teaching Council (Scotland) and are required during their initial teacher training to have covered the age range 3–12, with practical experience with each age group. The approval of courses of training is jointly the responsibility of the Scottish Office and GTC.
2 Primary education in Scotland covers seven years, from 5 to 12.
3 There is a single entry date to primary school in Scotland, namely the beginning of the school year, at which time all children enter school who will be five years of age by the end of February of that school year.
4 The teachers' contract in Scotland limits the size of classes in primary schools to 33 pupils, with an 'upper limit' of 39 and a 'maximum' of 25 in composite classes. Special schools and units have lower numbers.
5 Over 95 per cent of pupils attend education authority schools. By June 1996 there was only one self-governing primary school in Scotland receiving funding direct from central government.
6 There are many small primary schools; in some local authorities most of the primary schools have fewer than 100 pupils. There are over one hundred schools with 20 pupils or under.

RECOMMENDATIONS FOR PRIMARY EDUCATION IN 1965 AND SINCE 1987: A COMPARISON

Primary Education in Scotland (SED 1965) was prepared by a committee of teachers, college lecturers and members of Her Majesty's Inspectorate of Schools. It aimed to provide an appraisal of the best practices in primary schools and to contain valuable information and advice on methods, facilities and organisation in the classroom and the school. I have found it interesting to look back after thirty years at my annotated copy of the report and relate its recommendations to the current guidelines, as I was involved in its dissemination to both teachers in training and experienced teachers. The national guidelines for the 5–14 curriculum and assessment in Scotland and other papers from the Scottish Consultative Council on the Curriculum (SCCC) in the 1990s with regard to primary education have the following features in common with the Primary Memorandum of 1965:

The importance of continuity in a child's education; children's differing rates of development; and the importance of avoiding treating each subject as if it were a self-contained entity are all stressed.

The five curricular areas within which teaching and learning are set out within the current 5–14 Programme are similar to the areas discussed in the Memorandum in 1965 (in contrast to the discrete subjects within which the national curriculum is organised in England).

In the national framework set up in the 1990s there are suggested minimum percentages of time for each of these primary areas so that there is a proper balance between them. In a similar spirit to the Memorandum, time is left to the school's discretion, to allow for adjustments as children progress through the school and as individual needs arise and change.

The purposes of assessment set out show an appreciation of the continuous nature of development, the differing rates at which individual children reach these stages and the relationship of assessment to children's learning.

Problems about implementing curricular changes and providing adequate resources for small rural schools are considered.

There is a chapter in the Memorandum (SED 1965) on modern languages in the primary school; the points discussed there are relevant to current initiatives in primary schools.

In a chapter on Gaelic in the Memorandum the duty of schools in Gaelic-speaking areas not only to teach Gaelic as a subject in its own right but also to employ it as a means of instruction for Gaelic-speaking pupils in other subjects is stressed. A revival of interest in Gaelic in primary education in the last few years has been coupled with initiatives funded by the Scottish Office.

Thus recent developments in primary education in Scotland are not radically out of step with principles established over thirty years ago. This may well help to explain the more ready acceptance and implementation of the curriculum and related initiatives in Scotland in the 1990s. In England and Wales, in contrast, the national curriculum and related assessment are strikingly different from recent practice in primary education.

CURRICULUM AND ASSESSMENT IN PRIMARY EDUCATION: A POLICY FOR THE 1990s

Curricular developments

The government's wish to move towards a national curriculum, periodic national testing and greater accountability in schools is reflected in the developments over the past ten years in primary schools in Scotland, as it is in England and Wales. In 1987 a consultation paper was issued by the Secretary of State for Scotland entitled *Curriculum and Assessment in Scotland: A Policy for the 90s* (SED 1987), which claimed to identify a need for clearer and more structured advice on the balance between different components of the curriculum. Recognition was given, however, to curricular developments already underway for the age group 14–16. For that reason the focus for the new national guidelines was to be 5–14 (not 5–16 as in England). The consultation paper stated that national guidelines for the curriculum and for assessment in Scotland should ensure 'balance and breadth' under the already agreed headings of language arts, mathematics, environmental studies, expressive arts and religious education (including social and moral education). Concern was expressed to ensure not only balance and breadth, but also continuity on transfer from primary to secondary school. Thus already one can see a very different emphasis in Scotland with regard to the structure of the curriculum. In England and Wales, in contrast, the curriculum was divided into Core and other Foundation Subjects, with separate working groups to plan the curriculum within the different subject areas for the various 'Key Stages' 1–4.

In Scotland, by 1991 a series of working papers had been prepared by groups of professionals closely in touch with work in primary and secondary schools in the five following areas (related reports were also available or in preparation): English language, mathematics, environmental studies, expressive arts, and religious and moral education. After a period of consultation, national guidelines were published for each area based on the working-party reports. The working-party reports on the various curricular areas and on assessment were preceded by a general paper subtitled *The Balance of the Primary Curriculum* (SED 1989), in which minimum time allocations for the curriculum areas in the primary school were given, together with a 'flexibility element'. By 1993 the guidelines in all five curricular areas for 5–14 had been published by the Scottish Office Education Department (the renamed Scottish Education Department):

In 1991:
English language (listening, talking, reading and writing).
Mathematics (problem-solving and enquiry, information handling, number, money and measurement, shape, position and movement).

In 1992:
Expressive arts (including art and design, drama, music and physical education).
Religious and moral education (Christianity, other world religions and 'personal search').

In 1993:
Environmental studies (including science, social subjects, technology, health education and information technology).

A national guideline was also published in 1993 for personal and social development 5–14 (SOED 1993c).

The Structure and Balance of the Curriculum 5–14 (SOED 1993d) took account of the responses to the working paper of 1989, and developments in the Programme since then. It provides a useful overview of the Programme, intended to be helpful to schools in implementing the 5–14 curriculum. It lists the 'attainment outcomes' and 'strands' in the guidelines listed above. The following points are stressed:

- the principles governing the curriculum 5–14 are breadth, balance, coherence, continuity and progression for all pupils;
- the importance of the five curricular areas;
- the need for consideration of cross-curricular aspects;
- the structure of each of the national guidelines is intended to encourage the development of policies by individual schools and their implementation in the classroom;
- the starting point for assessment is to be the 'planned curriculum'.

Assessment is to be considered in terms of planning, recording, reporting and evaluating. To quote: 'Through these processes teachers gather information so that they can make professional judgements about pupils' progress and communicate these to pupils and parents' (SOED 1993d: 18).

A number of important features in the planning of the curricular proposals in Scotland differ from those in England:

1 Existing committees were charged with making the recommendations for the curriculum and assessment (not, as noted earlier, new committees as in England).
2 The membership of the working parties set up by the Scottish Consultative Council on the Curriculum reflected the wide range of professionals involved in education in schools, teachers in primary schools and subject specialists, headteachers from different types and sizes of schools, advisers and directors of education, college lecturers and representatives of the profession on secondment to SCCC. On the working parties was someone with expertise in the education of children with special needs, to whose educational needs attention was able to be paid.
3 A general framework is common to all the working papers and national guidelines; these include recommendations for attainment outcomes and targets and programmes of study.
4 These guidelines, which were published after a period of consultation, appear to have retained the main recommendations of the working parties.

5 In Scotland, following the publication of each guideline the schools have been encouraged to implement the proposals, with the aim of full implementation by 1998–9, without, as in England, being faced with amendments and revisions of the curriculum and the national tests within a very short time of their introduction.

6 Working-party reports on assessment and reporting, with a focus on improving classroom assessment and partnership with parents, were being issued for consultation at the same time as the curriculum documents.

Assessment within the primary school

In Scotland over the past ten years there have been two parallel developments in assessment.

General recommendations for assessment and reporting to parents have been linked with and built into the national guidelines; this assessment is an integral part of the national guidelines for the subject areas. Working-party reports on assessment have been followed by consultation and then national guidelines, on *Assessment 5–14* (SOED 1991a) and *Reporting 5–14* (SOED 1992c). Further documents to support these guidelines have been issued by SOED, including staff development packs, showing the importance accorded to the professional development of teachers in classroom assessment.

In addition to the above, there has been a programme of national tests, though in English and mathematics only. These tests were to be administered when the children had completed three years in primary school (that is, when they were eight years of age), and at the end of their primary schooling. The preparation of the national tests in Scotland was the responsibility of the Primary Assessment Unit in the Scottish Examination Board. The tests in English were to involve two tests of reading and two of writing. The reading tests were to be of comprehension, one of a narrative passage, one for information. The children were to write on a narrative and information topic and their writing was to be assessed for choice and use of language, selection and organisation of ideas and technical skills. The mathematics tests were to cover four units at a given level: problem-solving and enquiry; information handling; number, money and measurement; and shape, position and movement; these tasks also are set in different contexts. The teachers order the tests from a catalogue of tests at the level and on the topics they think appropriate for their pupils.

National testing has been controversial in Scotland, as in England and Wales. However, the teachers and parents in Scotland have succeeded in having the programme of national testing greatly modified. When the first round of national tests took place in Scotland in 1991, owing to parental and teacher opposition, only about half the children sat the tests. More flexibility as to the time of year at which the tests were to be conducted was then permitted. Subsequently the arrangements have been modified still further. The national tests form a back-up to teacher assessment and now need to be administered only when the teacher's own assessment indicates that the pupil has largely achieved the attainment at one level, not in any particular year in the primary school. Furthermore, there is reference in the documentation to the assessment of children with special educational needs as well as those for whom English is a second language. In 1992, a circular was issued confirming the revised arrangements, and stating that an individual pupil's performance in tests is to be communicated to the pupil and the parent. In short, league tables will not be compiled comparing pupil with pupil, or school with school on the basis of the testing. Indeed, with the present structure of the testing, and the tests themselves, no such comparisons would be possible. Thus, the national test data are used as a confirmation of teachers' professional judgement of the level attained in English and mathematics based on a wide range of classroom evidence. There is little evidence yet of the extent to which the teachers are indeed using the national tests within the revised, more flexible arrangements.

Attention has now turned to diagnostic assessment and the preparation of materials to assist teachers in making diagnostic assessment within the key areas of English, mathematics and science, under the general general title *Taking a Closer Look*. The Diagnostic Procedures project was funded by the Scottish Office Education Department and the Scottish Council for Research in Education, and the guidelines have been developed in collaboration with teachers. The project team and advisory committee were composed of staff from SCRE and colleges of education and from members of Her Majesty's Inspectorate. The booklets and related packages which link closely with the curricular developments within the 5–14 Programme are illustrated with examples from the classroom. They were made available free to all schools with the aim of helping teachers assess pupils' understanding and progress, and identify appropriate next steps (SCRE 1995).

DEVELOPMENTS IN PRIMARY EDUCATION IN ENGLAND: SOME CONTRASTS

Those familiar with the development of the national curriculum in England will appreciate how different are the curricular and assessment guidelines recommended for primary education in Scotland. In England subject committees were established whose members were chosen by the Secretary of State for Education. Each subject committee worked in isolation, leading inevitably to an overloading of the curriculum, particularly for primary schools at Key Stage 1. It is thus no surprise that radical revisions and a drastic slimming down should have proved essential. A crucial element within the development of the national curriculum in England has been the assessment at the end of each Key Stage (that is, in the primary school, when the children are about 7 and 11 years of age). The way that the assessment has developed, with an increasing focus on externally devised Standard Assessment Tasks (SATs), has resulted in the assessment driving the curriculum, possibly in inappropriate ways. Claims from teachers in England of pressures of work resulting from the national testing at the end of Key Stage 2 have led to external marking of scripts. The assessment is externally imposed at a particular point in time; the teachers are themselves not involved in the actual assessment of the scripts, receiving only the marked scripts without any diagnostic scoring on them; thus at most they can challenge the final mark. Recent documents from the School Curriculum and Assessment Authority (SCAA) are beginning to exhibit a greater commitment to recognising teachers in England as professionals and teacher assessment as fundamental to good teaching.

It would be naive to suggest that the plans for assessment formulated in Scotland in the 1980s and early 1990s were not politically driven, or that they were free from political interference; the same government was in power in Scotland over that period as in England and Wales. However, the criticisms made by the former chairmen of the committees in England and Wales could not so readily be levelled at the developments in Scotland. As noted earlier, national testing in Scotland in the primary school was only ever planned for English and mathematics and was to take place when the children had completed three years in school and were eight plus years of age; and league tables of the results of individual schools were not published. Furthermore, as a consequence of opposition even these plans have been modified. While teachers in Scottish primary schools have had to face the pressures of implementing the new curricular proposals, their colleagues in England have had to face the following additional pressures:

- publications by the former chairmen of the key committees on the curriculum and assessment criticising the way their reports have been interpreted;
- the greater emphasis on SATs rather than teacher assessment;
- the inclusion of assessment of mathematics and science for seven-year-olds as well as English, which left teachers with less time to spend on English, because of their insecurity in the other areas (science assessment at Key Stage 1 has now been dropped);
- attempts to compare schools' performance in the form of league tables, based on SATs, without any allowance for the very different starting points of the children, and in some schools, particularly in the inner cities, the large number of children for whom English is a second language. This last point has added to the political agenda in England the issue of 'value-added' assessment and currently, a proposal for compulsory Baseline Assessment of all children on entry to primary school.

In Scotland, in contrast to England, the national guideline for English language seems to give greater recognition to the diversity of culture and language within our community, and to a desire to foster respect for this in young children (see SOED 1991b). While reports on primary education by HMIs in Scotland have expressed concern at some aspects of language and writing, as was noted earlier, other aspects have received praise. There is concern about standards of literacy in Scotland and whether these are high enough, with a number of intervention projects underway with the aim of improving standards. There is also anxiety as to whether such projects are vulnerable with the current level of funding and the replacement of the large Regions by smaller councils. However, the surveys of literacy conducted within the Assessment of

Achievement Programme indicate that over the past twenty years, at least until 1992, there has been no decline in standards of literacy in primary schools. At the end of primary education (in Primary 7) there has been no change in either reading or writing; in Primary 4, there has been no change in reading and a slight fall in writing (Commission on Scottish Education 1996).

In England, English has been a high-profile subject politically, and one which has over recent years been subjected to a number of revisions. Claims have been made of falling standards; the methods employed to teach reading have been criticised, with demands for an increased emphasis on 'phonics'; claims have been made that there should be greater emphasis on spelling, grammar and punctuation, and on Standard English from early in the primary school. The curriculum proposed has been revised, and under threat of further revision over the ensuing years, as have been the assessment procedures. Those teaching English in primary schools in England have met not only with pressures from the proposals themselves and the national tests, the first when children are barely seven years of age. They have also been faced with frequent revisions. Research projects funded to analyse the effects of the changes were either barely completed, or the results were not yet widely available, before revisions to the curriculum and its assessment were considered. A recent review of the national curriculum and its assessment recommended that it be slimmed down, and that there should be no further changes for a period of five years.

In Scotland, the structure of the national guidelines, the fact that they cover broad areas and the fact that continuous assessment and improving teachers' assessment have been a major focus throughout the developments during 1990s have led to a more positive reaction by professionals to the developments. The extent to which these documents have so far influenced practice in primary schools in Scotland will be considered in the following section.

AN EVALUATION OF THE 5–14 PROGRAMME

The working parties planning the 5–14 Programme were set up from 1989; the first guidelines, those in English language and mathematics, were published in 1991; the final guidelines were published in 1993, and it is intended that the full 5–14 Programme will be in place in all areas of the curriculum by 1998–9. An independent evaluation of the implementation of the 5–14 Development Programme was funded by the Scottish Office Education and Industry Department (SOEID) between 1991 and 1995, with projects based at the Scottish Council for Research in Education, the University of Edinburgh, the University of Strathclyde and Northern College. A further two-year study is being sponsored by SOEID. The programme is set in context, and the main findings of the evaluation are reported in *Four Years of Change in Education 5–14* (Harlen 1996); a fuller report on the findings of the evaluation of the implementation in primary schools is to be found in *5–14 in the Primary School: The First Four Years* (Malcolm and Byrne 1996).

With regard to the curriculum, the researchers found that in primary schools initially implementation of the English language and mathematics guidelines had dominated the attention of the schools. However, by 1994 teachers appeared to have become familiar with the content and terminology of these and there was evidence of positive feelings towards them. As yet little progress had been made in implementation of the guidelines in the areas of religious and moral education, the expressive arts or environmental studies. The guidelines on environmental studies were regarded as helpful, making clear what was expected in this area and in planning to ensure that all aspects were covered. Headteachers were reported as regarding the guidelines as useful to ensure consistency of direction among staff and to help with staff development. A number of the teachers who were interviewed thought that 'their pupils were benefiting from a broader range of learning experiences, from the new emphasis on oral and problem-solving skills, and from a more consistent, continuous learning experience' (Malcolm and Byrne 1996: vi).

With regard to assessment, the researchers found that teachers tended to regard the specific guidelines on assessment as helpful. They appreciated the link in the guidelines between teaching and learning, and the opportunity they provided for reflection on assessment. During the period of the research the plans for the national testing in English and mathematics had to be modified as a consequence of opposition of teachers and parents. Many of those interviewed did not see the value of these tests and thought that they would merely encourage teaching to the test; some felt that they did not assess children's knowledge adequately.

In addition to balance and breadth in the curriculum, continuity was stressed as important in the 5–14 Programme. The researchers found some evidence of improved liaison between primary and nursery schools, helped, it was thought, by the 5–14 Programme. Primary-school staff expressed some satisfaction with links with secondary schools, though they felt that the contacts needed to be more orientated towards the curriculum. As will be seen in the following chapter there is limited evidence so far of impact of the 5–14 Programme on secondary schools, or that it has improved the continuity of children's learning when they move from primary to secondary school.

The evaluation reported here covers the early years of the implementation of the 5–14 Programme, mainly of the first two curricular guidelines to be introduced and the beginning of use of the assessment and reporting guidelines. Changes in the national testing announced at the end of 1992 were only beginning to be put into practice as the final data were collected. It will therefore be of interest to see what emerges from the evaluation in the years 1995–7. It is yet to be seen whether the changes so far will be sustained and what the impact will be on primary education in Scotland of the whole programme.

GAELIC-MEDIUM PRIMARY SCHOOLS

According to the 1991 census only 1.4 per cent of the population in Scotland over three years of age speak, read or write Gaelic. The largest concentrations are in the Western Isles, Highland and Strathclyde Regions; the remaining speakers are scattered throughout Scotland, with the largest single concentration in Edinburgh. However, it is only within the last ten years that education in Scotland through the medium of Gaelic in primary schools has shown a rapid increase, with support from the Scottish Office and Regional authorities. By 1996–7 there were 1,587 children in Gaelic-medium units in primary schools in Scotland. Many of the units are in small rural schools with composite classes; however, there are also units in Aberdeen, Edinburgh and Glasgow. For the first few years in primary school the curriculum may be delivered entirely through Gaelic; in the following years English will then be introduced gradually, with the aim that by the end of primary education the children will have equal fluency in Gaelic and English. Gaelic-medium education in Scotland is not

47

confined to Gaelic speakers, or those whose parents are Gaelic speakers; a child's attendance is a matter of parental choice. There has been a high level of support from parents whose children have been experiencing Gaelic-medium education. The 5–14 national guidelines are the basis for the education in these units as in other primary schools in Scotland. There is now a national guideline 5–14 for Gaelic, in English and in Gaelic, like the other reports, based on the recommendations of a working party; it parallels the report on English language 5–14 (SOED 1993b).

The Scottish Office has in recent years supported a range of initiatives in education (including Gaelic-medium units, resources, teacher education, broadcasting, the preparation of resources, and research), with grants to support Gaelic increasing dramatically over the last ten years. In April 1996 the Secretary of State for Scotland announced a further initiative with commitment until 1998, claiming that there has been impressive progress in developing Gaelic education in the past ten years, with good-quality education in the Gaelic-medium units. Research is currently funded by the Scottish Office to study the comparative attainment levels in Gaelic- and English-medium schools (due to be reported in 1999). A number of reports of relevance to Gaelic-medium teaching in primary schools have been published recently by the Leirsinn Research Centre on the Isle of Skye – on the use of Gaelic television programmes, on the critical skills needed for teaching in Gaelic-medium units, and on teacher training for Gaelic-medium education.

MODERN LANGUAGES IN THE PRIMARY SCHOOL

In recent years there have been national and Regional projects in many parts of Scotland involving the introduction of modern languages into primary schools; current plans are to extend this to all primary schools. The first phase started in 1989, with six secondary schools, each with a number of associated primary schools. In total the national pilot projects involved 12 secondary schools and 76 primary schools, covering four languages, with by 1993 over 4,000 pupils. An initiative by Strathclyde Region included a further 24 secondary schools and 133 primary schools. Most projects were in either French or German; one was in Italian and another in Spanish. In 1992 the Secretary of State announced that over the next five years a foreign language would be introduced into every primary school in Scotland. In the pilot projects secondary teachers visited associated primary schools and worked with their primary school colleagues. However, with the expansion of the provision the main burden will fall on primary teachers.

There is a general feeling that the pilot projects have been successful, particularly in promoting a favourable attitude to foreign languages. There is so far limited evidence on the longer-term effects on attainment in modern languages when pupils transfer to secondary school. A report by HM Inspectorate on the introduction of French into primary schools in Scotland in the 1960s noted that there was a lack of continuity on transition to secondary school and that many primary teachers lacked sufficient competence in the language. A number of issues still need to be resolved in this current venture if it is not to fail as did the earlier one – including whether there will be sufficient primary-school teachers with the necessary qualifications to provide the main input and whether they will be able to sustain such a venture in addition to the pressures involved with the full implementation of the 5–14 Programme. Attempts are being made to ensure that courses in modern languages are available for primary teachers and that there are sufficient resources. There is now more evidence on the value of bilingual education, and of commencing a second language at an early age. The relevance of mastery of at least one European language for employment in the European Community is also likely to give added impetus to projects such as these. (Further information on the research is available from the Scottish Centre for Information on Language Teaching and Research at the University of Stirling.)

STANDARDS AND QUALITY IN SCOTTISH PRIMARY SCHOOLS

Schools in Scotland are inspected by HM Inspectors (not by OFSTED as in England). Their programme of independent inspection evaluates and reports on the quality of education and the arrangements made by schools for assuring quality. *Standards and Quality in Scottish Schools 1992–95* (HMI 1996) assesses how well schools are performing in key aspects of their work across the three-year-period 1992–95. Scotland is now several years into an initiative in which schools are encouraged to take responsibility for their own quality assurance by evaluating their performance and by making the necessary changes.

The HMI report states that staff development is a strong feature in almost all primary schools. Most teachers are reported to be good at explaining and questioning and making their instructions and expectations clear to pupils, and at using varied teaching methods and providing well-chosen learning activities. Most pupils in primary schools are said to be industrious, well motivated and responsive to their teachers. Praise is given for 'the ethos' in primary schools: it is described as very good or good in over 90 per cent of schools. (See Chapter 8 for a fuller discussion of these issues.)

There is evidence from the HMI report that schools are beginning to implement the 5–14 Programme. However, there is still some way to go before it is fully implemented in all the main areas of the curriculum. It should be remembered, however, that the target is for that to happen by 1998–9 (and these inspections covered the years 1992–5).

The climate within which recent curricular and assessment initiatives in primary schools have developed is perhaps best summed up in a recent publication from the Scottish CCC, *Teaching for Effective Learning* (SCCC 1996), which immediately on publication won glowing tributes from teachers in Scotland, and overseas, according to a report in the *Times Educational Supplement Scotland* (see TES Scotland, 20 September 1996: 4). It is claimed that in the publication the Council has deliberately avoided prescriptive approaches. To quote:

> This paper is an attempt to act in partnership with teachers, to focus our joint professional enquiry upon the most important processes taking place in our schools – teaching and learning. . . . The reader will find in this paper no ringing endorsement of any one single best way to teach. The paper, and indeed CCC's whole initiative in this field, is at pains to recognise that teaching is a complex, difficult and challenging task, and that there are no easy answers. It is, however, an optimistic paper, premised upon the professional commitment of teachers to their vocation.
>
> (SCCC 1996: iii)

REFERENCES

Commission on Scottish Education (1996) *Learning to Succeed in Scotland: A Radical Look at Education Today and a Strategy for the Future*, Edinburgh: The Commission on Scottish Education.

DES (1967) *Children and their Primary Schools*, London: HMSO (the Plowden Report).

Harlen, W. (1996) *Four Years of Change in Education 5–14*, Edinburgh: SCRE.

HMI (1996) *Standards and Quality in Scottish Schools 1992-95*, Edinburgh: Audit Unit, SOEID.

Malcolm, H. and Byrne, M. (1996) *5–14 in the Primary School: The First Four Years*, Edinburgh: SCRE.

SCCC (1996) *Teaching for Effective Learning*, Dundee: SCCC.

SCRE (1995) *Taking a Closer Look: Education 5–14 Diagnostic Procedures*, Edinburgh: SCRE.
    Key Ideas in Diagnostic Assessment
    Taking a Closer Look at Reading
    Taking a Closer Look at Writing
    Taking a Closer Look at Number
    Taking a Closer Look at Information Handling
    Taking a Closer Look at Science

SED (1965) *Primary Education in Scotland*, Edinburgh: HMSO (the Primary Memorandum).

—— (1987) *Curriculum and Assessment in Scotland: A Policy for the 90s, A Consultation Paper*, Edinburgh: SED.

—— (1989) *Curriculum and Assessment in Scotland: A Policy for the 90's Paper 1, A Working Paper: The Balance of the Primary Curriculum*, Edinburgh: SED.

SOED Curriculum and Assessment in Scotland, National Guidelines:

SOED (1991a) *Assessment 5–14*, Edinburgh: HMSO.

—— (1991b) *English Language 5–14*, Edinburgh: HMSO.

—— (1991c) *Mathematics 5–14*, Edinburgh: HMSO.

—— (1992a) *Expressive Arts 5–14*, Edinburgh: HMSO.

—— (1992b) *Religious and Moral Education 5–14*, Edinburgh: HMSO.

—— (1992c) *Reporting 5–14*, Edinburgh: HMSO.

—— (1993a) *Environmental Studies 5–14*, Edinburgh: HMSO.

—— (1993b) *Gaelic 5–14*, Edinburgh: HMSO.

—— (1993c) *Personal and Social Development 5–14*, Edinburgh: HMSO.

—— (1993d) *The Structure and Balance of the Curriculum 5–14*, Edinburgh: HMSO.

4

THE STATUTORY YEARS OF SECONDARY EDUCATION

Change and progress

Brian Boyd

THE CONTEXT

Secondary schooling in Scotland has been organised on all-through, six-year comprehensive lines since the late 1960s. This chapter deals with the first four years of secondary education (age range 12–16) – the final years of statutory provision.

State education is the norm in Scotland. 'Private' (or 'public') schools account for less than 5 per cent of the pupil population, and to date only two secondary schools have 'opted out' of local authority control. The local authorities have traditionally been responsible for schooling and have developed a range of policies supported by strong advisory services. The size of Scotland has resulted in a largely consensual approach to educational policy-making, and the existence of central bodies such as the Scottish Examination Board, the Scottish Consultative Council on the Curriculum, the General Teaching Council and Her Majesty's Inspectorate working with local authority personnel has meant that secondary schooling has evolved in a more uniform fashion than elsewhere in the United Kingdom.

As confirmed in a recent review of the comprehensive system in the United Kingdom, *Thirty Years On* (Benn and Chitty 1996), secondary schools are, in the main, highly regarded in Scotland. They work hard, through the Guidance (pastoral) system, to support young people, particularly those at risk. Learning Support, a development from the previous 'remedial' departments, offers a sophisticated range of measures to support pupils with special educational needs, more of whom are now being integrated into mainstream schools. They also prepare young people effectively for the national examinations – Standard Grade at Secondary 4 and Higher Grade at Secondary 5 and 6. A higher proportion of young people in Scotland stay on beyond the statutory leaving age than in the United Kingdom as a whole and gain entrance qualifications for higher education. The introduction in the early 1980s of SCOTVEC awards has gone some way towards ensuring that young people of a non-academic bent who stay on are provided for. See Chapters 6 and 8 for more detail.

Subject teaching, by an all-graduate profession, is a key feature of secondary schools, although concerns continue to surface about under-achievement among young people from disadvantaged backgrounds (especially boys). Nevertheless, the efforts of secondary schools to have a positive ethos, to achieve high standards of attainment for all and to become more 'effective' make them the envy of the rest of the United Kingdom. As Boyd has argued, 'Education in Scotland has traditionally been associated with excellence' (1996).

But complacency is also a Scottish trait ('wha's like us?'), and we must be wary of giving the impression that everything is perfect. Problems have arisen nationally over the last few decades which have required national solutions. When they do arise, it has been the practice for secondary schooling to be reviewed in stages rather than, as in primary education, for an overall look to be taken at the sector as a whole. There have been reviews of Secondary (S) 3 and S4 in 1977, the upper school, S5 and S6, in 1981 and again in 1993, and S1 and S2 in 1986 and currently in the 5–14 Development Programme. The result has been a secondary system which struggles with the principles of 'continuity' and 'progression' but which has become more centralist in its structures across the country than at any time since comprehensivisation.

Even under strong local authorities, which, by developing their own policies and practices, gave the lie to the myth that in Scotland education is 'centrally governed and locally administered', there was a seemingly inexorable trend towards uniformity – subjects taught, timetabling structures and time allocations for subjects. The then Consultative Committee on the Curriculum (now Scottish CCC) contributed to this process with its publication of guidelines on curriculum structures whose recommendations became the expected norm. Indeed, the largest local authority, Strathclyde, went well beyond the CCC's advice and required all its secondary schools to adopt a thirty-period week, and, through its timetabling unit, gradually homogenised internal structures. When the Scottish Education Department in early 1983 produced its Action Plan for the 16-18 age group, Strathclyde demanded that all the schools 'harmonise' their timetables on an area basis to facilitate the movement of senior pupils among schools and FE colleges.

The pressure towards uniformity increased with the implementation in the mid 1980s of the Technical and Vocational Education Initiative (TVEI), which sought to give pupils an 'entitlement curriculum' and which demanded guarantees from the schools of minimum time allocations for areas of the curriculum in return for funding. The final piece in the jigsaw has been the publication of examination results in terms of raw data which can be converted, by the press and others, into 'league tables'. One of the repercussions of this has been to push many secondary schools towards an eight Standard Grade structure in a bid to improve their performance in these league tables. Thus, while the overall standard of attainment in secondary schools, as measured by examination results, has risen steadily over the last two decades, it can be argued that it has been at the expense of flexibility and diversity, at least in the structure of the curriculum and, increasingly, teaching methods.

Another influence on the system is that of Her Majesty's Inspectorate, still a potent force in Scotland. As well as their published reports of individual school inspections, their drive for improvements in learning and teaching has lead them to produce a series of influential publications, not least *The Education of Pupils with Learning Difficulties* (SED 1978), a whole series with the title *Effective Learning and Teaching* including *Effective Secondary Schools* (SED 1988) and *The Education of Able Pupils P6 to S2* (SOED 1993). All these sought to take a balanced view of what constitutes 'good practice' based on inspections, and were welcomed by the profession. More recently, the Inspectorate has entered more contentious areas and has chosen to take what many (including myself) see as a partisan position. Thus, in *Achievement for All* (SOEID 1996) the Inspectors have recommended that all secondary schools introduce 'setting' by attainment in S1 and S2 on the basis of 5–14 Levels – a view rejected by sections of the profession and other stakeholders as unsupported by research or practice.

Thus, albeit from a strong base of public and professional support, Scottish secondary education has faced a series of real challenges, not least the discontinuity between primary and secondary school and reform of the assessment and certification system, first at S3 and S4, and more recently in S5 and S6. Politically, under-achievement, especially among working-class boys, has emerged as a concern nationally, and the task of improving learning and teaching has been carried out against a backdrop of examination league tables and parental choice of school.

THE EARLY YEARS – FRESH START VERSUS CONTINUITY AND PROGRESSION

In Scotland, secondary schooling begins after seven years of primary education. The move from one sector to the other is characterised by change – in terms of the structure of the curriculum (5 'areas' become 15+ subjects); the pattern of learning and teaching (one teacher with flexibility to plan the shape of the day to 15+ teachers who see the pupils for between one and four hours per week); the status of the pupils (from responsible, increasingly independent learners to 'juniors' with little voice in the system). It has often been argued that the primary school is a child-centred, caring place while the secondary is a subject-centred 'examination factory', and while this is untrue as a generalisation of either sector, it does bring into sharp relief the differences in ethos between the two. A recent survey of teachers' views, carried out as part of the Improving School Effectiveness Project (SOEID in progress) has indicated that on many issues – views of pupils as learners; staff–management relationships; morale, etc. – primary teachers are more optimistic than their secondary counterparts. These differences are not new or surprising to most people in education in Scotland, and, indeed, lie at the heart of the 5–14 Development Programme's drive for progression and continuity.

In 1993, Her Majesty's Inspectorate, in their report *The Education of Able Pupils P6 to S2* (SOED 1993), asserted that 'The fresh start approach in S1 is no longer tenable.' Almost a decade previously, the Consultative Committee on the Curriculum set up a committee to address the problems of discontinuity which produced its Discussion Paper *Education 10–14 in Scotland* (CCC 1986). In the eyes of many in the education community, this was a radical and enlightened report, advocating 'autonomy within professional guidelines' for teachers to devise appropriate curricula for their pupils, and stressing the importance of high expectations in its now famous phrase 'the classroom crackles with subliminal signals'. But, as Boyd has argued (1992), the report came at the wrong time. A protracted period of teacher industrial action had just ended, and the new Education Minister was in no mood to allow the profession to block curricular change again. A new era of 'accountability', of 'standards' and of national 'benchmarking' had arrived – and from and out of this grew the 5–14 Development Programme.

The 5–14 Programme was an exercise in damage limitation, with the educational 'policy community', as McPherson has described it in *Governing Education* (McPherson and Raab 1988), or the 'Leadership Class', the term preferred by Humes (1986), struggling to make something positive out of the ideological paper *Curriculum and Assessment in Scotland: A Policy for the 90s* (SED 1987). The 5–14 Programme duly emerged, and it tried to address the needs not only of the primary sector but the first two years of secondary – and the vexed issues of continuity and progression. It did so by producing a set of guidelines for all areas of the primary curriculum and extending these into S1 and S2. It even produced, in *The Structure and Balance of the Curriculum 5–14* (SOED 1993), a diagram showing the 5 *curricular areas* of the primary neatly interfacing with the 8 *modes* of the secondary. But, it failed to address the reality that in S1 and S2 the curriculum is not organised into 8 modes as it is in S3 and S4. It is organised into some 15 subjects (English; mathematics; history; geography; modern studies; science; modern languages; art and design; technology; physical education; religious and moral education; personal and social development; music; drama – with some schools offering computing, more than one modern language, etc.). Thus, continuity and progression can be said to be more apparent than real.

There is an apparent alphabetical continuity in the assessment system: pupils can progress through Levels A–E of 5–14 and move into the Standard Grade system in the middle years of secondary, which has the letters F (Foundation) and G (General) as two of the three levels of awards. However, the third and 'highest' award is

Credit, thus breaking the sequence and confirming that the continuity was more a product of accident than design. In fact, no pupil achieving Level E by S2 would ever follow a Foundation course in that subject.

Nevertheless, the assessment guidelines of the 5–14 Programme are widely regarded as being the most helpful of all to teachers. The challenge facing the secondary school now is not the lack of appropriate assessment information accompanying the child from primary to secondary – confined in the past to numerical information on English and mathematics – but the prospect of information overload. Theoretically, when 5–14 is fully implemented, pupils will have been assessed over seven years across some 100 strands within the 5–14 Programme. Supplemented and confirmed by the results of national testing, this information will be transferred to the secondary – and it must, if 5–14's aims are to be realised, inform learning and teaching in S1 and S2. No longer will there be any excuse for the 'fresh start', and teachers cannot continue to treat every S1 cohort as if it were the 'same as last year's'.

LEARNING AND TEACHING IN THE FIRST TWO YEARS OF SECONDARY

Since comprehensive schooling was introduced in Scotland in the mid 1960s, the first two years of secondary have been seen as a 'common course' with all pupils following the same curriculum in mixed ability classes. While mixed ability teaching has remained a contentious issue, most local authorities in Scotland had policies which ensured that, at least in S1, there was mixed ability organisation. Strathclyde Regional Council pioneered the 'member/officer' approach to policy-making, with elected representatives and officials working together in committees. The *Report on the First Two Years of Secondary School* (SRC 1981), produced by such a committee, contained a 'Note of Dissent' signed by councillors and headteachers, which rejected mixed ability teaching in S2 because of the lack of any 'mass of incontestable evidence' to support such an approach. Nevertheless, mixed ability became the policy, though in many schools it was more honoured in the breach than in the observance.

Far more important than the form of organisation, it can be argued, is the pedagogy which accompanies it. In 1996, the

Scottish CCC published a paper called *Teaching for Effective Learning* (SCCC 1996), which was the culmination of the debate begun in the 1960s. It argued that 'the reflective professional' must be prepared to engage with theory and research, and questioned the 'orthodoxies' which had become entrenched in the secondary school. The model of staff development and in-service training in Scotland under strong local authorities always had the tendency to emphasise the 'how to' rather than the 'why' questions. The 'delivery' model of centralised packages (which, as we will see, characterised the Standard Grade initiative) or commercially produced schemes began to dominate, so much so that 'forward planning', for long a key feature of the primary teacher's approach, largely disappeared from S1 and S2, and subjects, as they moved away from reliance on whole-class teaching, began to find new, but often equally narrow, methodologies.

Mathematics, about which now there is great concern over standards of attainment, is a good case in point. It went for 'individualised learning', often through commercial schemes, and learning became a silent, solitary process for many pupils. For the teachers, teaching became 'marking', and the interaction between teacher and learner and among learners seemed to diminish. In other subjects, methodologies such as 'resourced-based learning' (RBL), 'core + extensions' and small-group teaching emerged as 'solutions' to the challenges posed by mixed ability classes. Taken as a range of strategies, they would have offered a flexible approach to differentiation – which had become the key challenge for schools. But it was the rigid adherence to one method or another which began in the 1980s and 1990s to cause disquiet, and has led to the current emphasis by HMI, the Scottish CCC and local authorities on the wider issue of 'effective learning and teaching'.

One of the problems which emerged was the ubiquitous worksheet – and 'death by a thousand worksheets' became a familiar description of secondary education, from S1 to S4. The worksheet had emerged in the 1970s as a useful tool to allow the teacher to meet a range of needs in the mixed ability class. Properly devised and used, it remains a key part of planning for learning. However, as they proliferated, their impact became, potentially, negative. The problems of 'sameness', of a lack of continuous writing expected of pupils and, most worrying of all, a belief that the worksheet was almost a teacher-proof approach began to raise concerns that teachers were in danger of being de-skilled and that pupils were not being challenged. In the wake of the HMI report on able pupils (SOED 1993), a study of schools entitled *Towards a Climate of Achievement* (McMichael and Boyd 1993) suggested that able pupils were being fed a diet of 'extension worksheets' and were not being challenged. The same study, and others, reinforced the fact that the overwhelming view of pupils in S1 or S2 was that, while they liked the variety of secondary, they were doing work they had already done, were not being challenged, were not regarded as independent learners and did not feel that they were given any responsibility for their own learning.

S3 AND S4 – THE STANDARD GRADE YEARS

While the first two years of secondary education remain for many the area where learning is least satisfactory, there is increasing concern among the profession that the whole of secondary education is too centralised. The structure of the third and fourth year of the secondary curriculum varies little across the country. Since the 'O Grades' were replaced in the early 1980s by Standard Grade, thereby opening up for the first time the possibility of certification for all, schools have tended to operate a timetabling structure which commonly enables pupils to take 7 or 8 Standard Grade subjects. The 'core' has been expanded to some 90 per cent of the pupils' timetable, and time allocation is the subject of national guidelines.

However, it must be said that the Standard Grade programme was widely welcomed by the profession. The S3 and S4 curriculum in the early comprehensive schools was often simply a replication of the old senior secondary (grammar school) and junior secondary (secondary modern) structures. Schools timetabled S3 and S4 in two blocks, certificate and non-certificate, and a significant proportion of the population emerged after eleven years of schooling with no certification of any kind. However, by the 1970s, comprehensive schools were challenging this division. In some parts of Scotland, the Certificate in Secondary Education (CSE) was introduced to ensure that there was a challenge for the less 'academic' pupils. In most, however, there was simply a year-on-year increase in the numbers of pupils being presented for

O Grades, an examination originally designed for some 30–40 per cent of the population.

Something had to give, and in 1974 a wide-ranging review of the system in S3 and S4 (and beyond) was undertaken by what became known as the Munn, Dunning and Pack committees. They looked, respectively, at the structure of the curriculum (*The Structure of the Curriculum in the Third and Fourth Years of the Scottish Secondary School*, SED 1977b), assessment and certification (*Assessment for All: Report of the Committee to Review Assessment in the Third and Fourth Years of Secondary Education in Scotland*, SED 1977a) and truancy and indiscipline across the whole of secondary (*Truancy and Indiscipline in Schools in Scottish Secondary Schools*, SED 1977c). They deliberated and consulted and in 1977 reported. Munn largely reinforced the Hirstian, subject-based curriculum, with a nod in the direction of cross-curricular courses, but only for the less able. However, it has been argued, the Hirstian view of the curriculum does not fit easily with a more integrated approach to learning in the primary school.

Dunning purposed a new system of national assessment and certification which incorporated some element of internal assessment and which offered the possibility for all pupils of certification at one of three levels – Foundation, General and Credit. A feasibility study was undertaken and the proposals were implemented, albeit interrupted by the industrial action in the early 1980s, caused not by opposition to the changes but by concerns about overload. Indeed, the implementation of Standard Grades was a model of what Gatherer (1990) has called the Scottish 'classical' approach to curriculum development. Local authorities took the lead in particular subjects and allocated advisers to form writing teams with teachers and HMI, and the whole thing worked smoothly in the main.

In Scottish secondary schools, the 'subject choice' or 'options' process begins mid-way through the pupils' second year. Often subjects are jostling for position and trying to ensure that they get their fair share of the able pupils. While this may seem unprofessional, the publication of examination results and the production each year of 'relative ratings', in which subject departments have their performance compared to that of others within the school (and in other similar schools), has ensured that this will continue to be a reality. The pupil must take English; mathematics; a social subject (history; geography; modern studies); a modern language; at least one science; a creative and aesthetic subject (art; drama; music; PE) and a technology subject (computing; technological studies; home economics). Thus the 'core' takes up some 90 per cent of the pupil's week, and while there is choice within some of these core areas, once religious and moral education, PE and social education are added, there is little time for further choice. The two principles of breadth and choice come into conflict, and pupil motivation in some of the subjects which have been recently added to the core, for example, modern languages, in some cases suffers as a result of what is seen as compulsion.

The typical approach to S3 and S4 in Scottish schools is for pupils to follow 7 or 8 Standard Grade courses. Theoretically, the pupil will find his or her own level and will be in a mix of Foundation, General and Credit sections. The original intention of the Dunning committee was that final decisions about which level of examination the pupils would sit would be left as late as possible, and each pupil sits papers at two contiguous levels so that options are kept open. However, the drive towards earlier internal selection makes this problematic, and those subjects which have the facility within the timetable to do so feel under pressure to 'set' by attainment earlier and earlier.

The issue of the balance of internal assessment and external examination has never achieved consensus, with the external continuing to dominate. Similarly, the issue of coursework has raised fears that pupils from disadvantaged areas are discriminated against, so much so that Strathclyde Regional Council devoted a substantial budget to the setting up of study support centres designed as part of its anti-poverty strategy to give pupils from such areas access to a place to study, information technology and the support of an adult tutor. In recent years, other authorities in Scotland, with the support of the Prince's Trust – Action, have set up new models of study support including summer schemes, to combat the effects of disadvantage. In 1994, the SOED distributed to all secondary schools in Scotland a copy of a multi-media support pack on study support produced for the Prince's Trust by the Quality in Education Centre at the University of Strathclyde (*A Place for Success* (MacBeath *et al.* 1994)).

The *Higher Still: Opportunity for All* initiative will be dealt with in the following chapter, but it is worth noting that it is predicated on the assumption that the 5–14 Development Programme will result in increased attainment. Indeed, the Howie committee, which preceded the Higher Still Programme, even suggested that in time Standard Grades might be taken at the end of the pupils' third year rather than the fourth. This was too radical a proposal for many, and has since been dropped. However, the question remains – will 5–14 promote improvements in pupil learning which in turn will result in higher achievement at Standard Grade?

SOME KEY ISSUES IN SCOTTISH SECONDARY SCHOOLING

Secondary schools across the United Kingdom have become the focus of political attention, and issues such as selection, opting out of local authority control, and, ultimately, the future of comprehensive schools themselves have been the subject of debate. Celebrated cases have always been used to give weight to one side of the argument, and the recent closure of 'failing schools' in England, the débâcle of the Ridings school, and the decision of a front-bench Labour spokesperson to send her child to an opted-out, grant-maintained school have focused attention on school effectiveness. In Scotland the debate is a different one, with virtually no opted-out schools, with a strong history of 'omnibus' schools long before comprehensivisation and with a great measure of popular support for state, non-selective education.

Secondary schools may well be less flexible in their structures than elsewhere in the United Kingdom, but the overall standards of attainment, of support and of perceived effectiveness are higher. There are few if any 'failing schools' in Scotland, though there are some which, because of demographic issues and the effects of parental choice, may find themselves with a disproportionate number of pupils from areas of disadvantage and experience the associated problems of under-achievement and low aspirations.

In 1993, the Scottish Office Education (and Industry) Department (SOEID) funded the largest school effectiveness/school improvement research project in Scottish education. A team from the University of Strathclyde and the Institute of Education at the University of London are working with eighty schools across Scotland looking at pupils' progress in the cognitive and affective domains, and its relationship with the actions which schools take to manage change. The search is on for the Holy Grail of 'value-added', in other words the effect which *the school* has on the pupils' progress as opposed to that contributed by the family, socio-economic status and other factors outwith the school. In other words, if Rutter's conclusions in *Fifteen Thousand Hours* (Rutter *et al.* 1979) that schools can make a difference are right, the question is what is it that they do which can be shown to have a positive effect on pupil progress?

School improvement is the goal, and the main difference between the Scottish approach and that of the rest of the United Kingdom is its commitment to self-evaluation. HMI in Scotland claim to have worked hard over the last decade to create a 'quality culture'. In the secondary sector this has involved the publication of a series of ring-bound folders each with the aim of helping schools with self-evaluation. Thus, advice on the use of examination results, ethos indicators and performance indicators have all been couched in these supportive terms. In addition, the promotion of school development planning and staff development and appraisal have, HMI would argue, helped make secondary schools become better managed.

Secondary schools in Scotland are very hierarchical organisations. An average-size school of 800 pupils will have a management structure of a Headteacher, a Depute Headteacher, 3 Assistant Headteachers, around 16 Principal Teachers (Subject), 3 or 4 Principal Teachers (Guidance), a number of Assistant Principal Teachers in the larger departments and in Guidance, 3 or 4 Senior Teachers and the rest classroom, or unpromoted, teachers. As head of a small secondary school in the 1980s where the roll had fallen in line with demographic trends, I myself had a pupil population of around 500 and a staff of 42, of whom 27 were in promoted posts. Contrast this with a similar-sized primary with 550 pupils and 23 staff, only 6 of them in promoted posts.

These structures have their origins in reports published in the late 1960s and early 1970s which addressed two problems, namely the lack of promotion prospects for newly appointed teachers and the fear that pupils in large secondary schools – 2,000 was a normal roll in secondaries in the 1970s – would have no one who knew them by name. Both these problems have largely disappeared. There is an over supply of teachers in secondary schools, and the average size of comprehensive schools is now around 800 pupils. What is more, it has become increasingly clear that schools, as more funding is devolved to them, wish to have greater flexibility in management structures, often creating faculties rather than departments and creating cross-curricular posts. With the concern over 'departmentalism', excessive 'boundary maintenance' and fragmentation of the curriculum in S1 and S2, there may well be a need for a radical review of the management structures of schools.

This will face opposition from vested interests initially, but in the longer term it may free secondary schools from what some have called the 'cult of managerialism' which has sought to treat them as businesses or factories, introducing practices such as 'audit', 'development planning', 'target setting' and 'appraisal'. Schools have been subject to 'quality assurance' which has increasingly emphasised the *measurable* aspects of their work. The language of the market place has infiltrated the staffroom and the drive has been to achieve effectiveness by increasing efficiency. This managerialism has led to principal teachers becoming 'middle managers' and those above the rank of assistant headteacher becoming the 'senior management team'.

There is evidence now of a refocusing on the classroom, the process of learning and teaching, the sharing of good practice and, within the context of the 5–14 Development Programme, a belief that the cluster of schools may be the most appropriate unit for improving learning and teaching. This trend may well require a change both in structure and in government policy since the principle of parental choice of school often conflicts with continuity and progression between primaries and their associated secondary school.

THE SCOTTISHNESS OF THE SYSTEM

Teachers in Scottish schools have had a nationally agreed contract since the 1970s which, in the secondary sector, guarantees unpromoted staff a minimum of four hours' non-pupil-contact time. Class sizes have fixed maximum limits of 33 in S1 and S2 for classroom subjects and 20 for practical, and 30 and 20 respectively from S3 onwards. Schools are funded on a 'real cost' basis (not by 'formula' as in England and Wales), HMI have resisted any moves to go down the OFSTED route, and there is a General Teaching Council to maintain standards in the profession.

Nevertheless, the publication of Her Majesty's Inspectorate reports on schools and of examination results, as well as costs per pupil and attendance (and exclusion) statistics in a form susceptible to conversion to 'league tables', has brought accountability to the fore. Some have argued that the result is that we now 'value what we measure rather than measure what we value', but whatever one's standpoint, it is incontrovertible that concerns over what Gray *et al.* (1983) called 'downward incrementalism' have been raised. The phenomenon of the wash-back effect of examination syllabuses to the early years has given rise to the fear that when Higher Still is implemented, secondary schools will disengage with 5–14, turning it into 5–12 and thus making continuity and progression more difficult to attain. Similarly, the pressure on schools to do well in the examination league tables may have the effect of causing schools to rely more and more on 'setting' by attainment and employing more 'formal' teaching methods. Thus, in an attempt to raise standards, organisational remedies are being offered to what are problems of teaching methods, motivation and low aspirations.

As we look forward to the millennium, there are still challenges to be faced in Scottish secondary schools. A new paradigm may be required to take account of issues such as 'multiple intelligences' (Gardner 1993), 'emotional intelligence' (Goleman 1996), 'accelerated learning' (Jensen 1994) and the impact of information technology on learning and teaching. If raising achievement is the aim, then a structure which sticks rigidly to age-stage divisions, which relies solely on 'subjects' as the building blocks and which still seeks to categorise pupils by present (cognitive) attainment may need to undergo a more radical revision than has taken place since the War.

Perhaps the monolithic all-through, six-year school, organised on age-stage lines and with every child proceeding in a lock-step manner through the system, is not appropriate for the twenty-first century. Rather than concentrate on building and structures, perhaps we need to start with *learning* and seek to provide the most flexible system possible to help young people learn more effectively.

REFERENCES

Benn, C. and Chitty, C. (1996) *Thirty Years On: Is the Comprehensive School Alive and Well or Struggling to Survive?*, London: David Fulton.

Boyd, B. (1992) 'Letting a hundred flowers blossom', Unpublished Ph.D. thesis, Glasgow University.

—— (1996) 'Scottishness of our schools', *The Herald*, 28 August.

CCC (1986) *Education 10–14 in Scotland*, Edinburgh: CCC.

Gardner, H. (1993) *Multiple Intelligences: The Theory in Practice*, London: HarperCollins.

Gatherer, W. (1990) *Curriculum Development in Scotland*, Professional Issues in Education, Edinburgh: Scottish Academic Press.

Goleman, D. (1996) *Emotional Intelligence*, London: Bloomsbury.

Gray, J., McPherson, A. and Raffe, D. (1983) *Reconstructions of Secondary Education: Theory, Myth and Practice since the War*, London: Routledge and Kegan Paul.

Humes, W. M. (1986) *The Leadership Class in Scottish Education*, Edinburgh: John Donald.

Jensen, E. (1994) *The Learning Brain*, California: Turning Point Publishing.

MacBeath, J., Boyd, B. and Newall, F. (1994) *A Place for Success*, Quality in Education, University of Strathclyde, Glasgow.

McMichael, P. and Boyd, B. (1993) *Towards a Climate of Achievement*, Quality in Education, University of Strathclyde, Glasgow.

McPherson, A. and Raab, C. (1988) *Governing Education: A Sociology of Policy since the War*, Edinburgh: Edinburgh University Press.

Rutter, M., Maughan, B., Mortimore, P., Ouston, J. and Smith, A. (1979) *Fifteen Thousand Hours: Secondary Schools and their Effects on Children*, London: Open Books.

SCCC (1996) *Teaching for Effective Learning*, SCCC: Dundee.

SED (1977a) *Assessment for All: Report of the Committee to Review Assessment in the Third and Fourth Years of Secondary Education in Scotland* (the Dunning Report), Edinburgh: HMSO.

—— (1977b) *The Structure of the Curriculum in the Third and Fourth Years of the Scottish Secondary School* (the Munn Report), Edinburgh: HMSO.

—— (1977c) *Truancy and Indiscipline in Scottish Secondary Schools* (the Pack Report), Edinburgh: HMSO.

—— (1978) *The Education of Pupils with Learning Difficulties in Secondary Schools in Scotland*, Edinburgh: HMSO.

—— (1983) *16–18 Action Plan*, Edinburgh: HMSO.

—— (1987) *Curriculum and Assessment in Scotland: A Policy for the 90s*, Edinburgh: HMSO.

—— (1988) *Effective Secondary Schools*, Edinburgh: HMSO.

SOED (1993) *The Education of Able Pupils P6 to S2*, Edinburgh: HMSO.

—— (1993) *The Structure and Balance of the Curriculum 5–14*, Edinburgh: HMSO.

SOEID (1995) *Higher Still – Opportunity for All*, Edinburgh: HMSO.

—— (1996) *Achievement for All*, Edinburgh: HMSO.

Strathclyde Regional Council (1981) *Report on the First Two Years of Secondary School*, Glasgow: SRC.

5

UPPER-SECONDARY EDUCATION

David Raffe

INTRODUCTION

There are several paradoxes at the heart of Scottish upper-secondary education. Other countries admire its alleged breadth and high standards, the high proportion of school leavers it sends on to university, and its pioneering modular system of vocational education; but within Scotland it is seen to be failing and in need of reform. It is embarking on a reform introduced by a Conservative government with the support of industry and the political right; but this reform will extend comprehensive education and is inspiring left-wing reformers south of the Border. The reform is one of the most radical and far-reaching attempted in any country at this level of education; but it has been moulded by vested interests, embodies an evolutionary strategy of change, and may yet fail to challenge the deep-rooted conservatism of Scottish secondary education.

The reform, Higher Still, will introduce a unified system of upper-secondary education in 1999. It is too soon in 1997 to predict its success or its impact on Scottish education. Yet it is no longer possible to write about upper-secondary education in Scotland without giving Higher Still a central place. In this chapter I first describe the system of the mid 1990s, many of whose key features will persist after 1999, and the students who enter it. I then outline the weaknesses of this system, the debates which led to the publication of *Higher Still* in 1994, and the main features of the system which it will introduce. Finally, I discuss Higher Still in relation to other possible reform strategies, and suggest why a unified system was adopted. In the process I hope to explain the paradoxes listed above.

UPPER-SECONDARY EDUCATION: THE EMERGENCE OF A STAGE

Most secondaries have an 'upper school', but the term 'upper-secondary education' was not used much before the Howie committee adopted it in 1992. Until recently the fifth and sixth years of secondary school (S5 and S6) did not comprise a very substantial or distinct stage of Scottish education. Only a minority of students stayed on, and most of these left after a year. In many schools voluntary stayers were outnumbered by 'winter leavers', students who had to stay on for the first term of S5 because they were too young to leave after S4. Many S5 students took S4 courses. Most students who stayed on continued at the same school; Scotland has no equivalent of the Sixth Form College or Tertiary College.

However, S5 and S6 are becoming a more distinct stage of Scottish education. More students stay on voluntarily at school, and they stay there longer. There is a clearer break with S4, and few S5 students continue with S4 courses. Higher Still will place all S5 and S6 courses within a single framework, and emphasise the break with the compulsory school years. But while the boundary between compulsory and upper-secondary schooling gets stronger, in the longer term this will be balanced by an increasingly flexible boundary between upper-secondary schooling and cognate provision in further, higher and continuing education.

STUDENTS IN UPPER-SECONDARY EDUCATION

About three-quarters of Scottish sixteen-year-olds stay on voluntarily in full-time education beyond the end of S4. The vast majority of these – 70 per cent of the year group in 1995–6 – stay on at school, and the remaining 5 per cent enter full-time further education (FE) (Scottish Office 1996: 6; Lynn 1996: 25). Winter leavers account for a further 10 per cent or so of the year group. School staying-on rates have been rising since the 1970s, more continuously than in England, where periods of rapid expansion have alternated with periods of stability.

Most young people stay on at school for instrumental reasons, to get qualifications for higher education or a job. More young people are staying on because the incentives to do so have become stronger: there are more places in higher education to aim for and employers are demanding higher credentials. Conversely, the decline in the youth labour market and the continued risk of unemployment has reduced the incentive to leave school at sixteen. Other factors have contributed to rising staying-on rates. More young people are from middle-class homes and have better-educated parents, factors traditionally associated with higher educational aspirations and with staying on. Rising Standard Grade attainments in S4 have encouraged more people to stay on to S5 to build on their success. Young people's main reasons for staying on are instrumental, but a growing proportion say that they stay on also because they enjoy school life, or wish to study particular courses or subjects (Paterson and Raffe 1995).

Staying-on rates to S6 (at seventeen years) have risen even faster, proportionately, than staying on to S5. Between 1985 and 1995 the proportion of each year group staying on voluntarily to S5 rose from 46 to 70 per cent, while the proportion staying on to S6 rose from 21 to 43 per cent (Scottish Office 1996: 6). In the mid 1980s only a minority of voluntary stayers to S5 subsequently continued into S6; by the mid 1990s a majority stayed on to S6 and upper-secondary schooling is increasingly a two-year stage. This largely reflects the influence of higher education. It is possible to enter higher education from S5, and about 5 per cent of each age group do so, but most young people need two post-compulsory years to gain the qualifications for admission to higher education.

Most students with good Standard Grade attainment stay on as a matter of course, while those with poor attainments tend to see little point in continuing at school. This is changing slowly, and staying-on rates have risen fastest among the least qualified. As more young people stay on, S5 students are becoming more heterogeneous. However, in one important respect they are becoming more homogeneous: a growing proportion has aimed to enter further or higher education, and at least up to the mid 1990s a growing proportion has succeeded in doing so. Despite the expansion of the upper-secondary school, it is not the terminal stage of education for most students (Surridge and Raffe 1995).

UPPER-SECONDARY COURSES AND QUALIFICATIONS IN THE MID 1990s

The distinctive features of courses in S5 and S6 are flexibility (most courses are short or modular and permit year-on-year decision-making) and the absence of tracks. The main components of the S5 curriculum are 'academic' Highers and 'vocational' National Certificate (NC) modules; but instead of being channelled into one or other of these most students take both, in varying proportions.

The Higher is the principal upper-secondary course, and the main qualification for higher education. It is a subject-based course, traditionally taken over one year, although it is often offered over two years to students with modest attainments in the subject at Standard Grade. A high-attaining student with six or seven Standard Grades at Credit level is likely to study five Highers in S5. Since three Highers are the notional minimum requirement for university entrance, the equivalent of two A levels in the rest of the United Kingdom, this student could qualify for university after only one post-compulsory year. However, even able students find the step up from Standard Grade to Higher a difficult one, and most students take fewer than five Highers in S5, often only one or two, and they use NC modules to fill the gaps.

The National Certificate is a national system of modules, each of a notional forty hours' duration, available in schools, colleges and other centres. It was introduced in 1984, when it replaced nearly all non-advanced vocational courses in Scotland. The Action Plan which introduced it (Scottish Education Department 1983) was a wide-ranging reform. It rationalised provision within a single modular framework, updated the curriculum and promoted more progressive approaches to teaching, learning and assessment. It was primarily intended as a reform of FE, but the NC modules, which covered most of the general curriculum as well as occupationally specific fields, proved unexpectedly successful in schools. Most S5 and S6 students take at least one module, and NC students in schools outnumber NC students in FE colleges. Modules are variously used in schools to provide short pro-grammes for winter leavers, as an alternative to Highers for lower-attaining students, in conjunction with Highers (as a bridge or safety-net), to extend the Highers curriculum (adding vocational enhancements and interest courses or filling small gaps in the timetable), or to deliver areas of the curriculum where Highers certification was unavailable or inappropriate (Weir and Kydd 1991; Croxford *et al.* 1991). Modules also fill the gap left by the phasing-out of O Grades since the late 1980s. Previously many S5 students had resat S4 O Grades, or attempted new O Grade subjects, often alongside Highers (McPherson 1984); Standard Grade courses are less suited for S5 study and students are more likely to take modules instead. Despite the wide take-up of modules in schools, few S5 or S6 students study programmes composed mainly of NC modules. The role of modules is largely secondary to that of Highers, and they tend to be seen as second-class (Croxford *et al.* 1991). Their value as credentials is uncertain, and the difference in status between Highers and modules is reinforced by differences in curriculum design, pedagogy and assessment.

Students who stay on to S6 take varying combinations of Highers (either new subjects or subjects started in S5 and taken over two years), NC modules and courses leading to the Certificate of Sixth Year Studies (CSYS). The CSYS is a post-Higher course, designed to promote independent study and to help students prepare for university. However, it is not normally recognised as a university entrance qualification and for this reason has had a somewhat problematic status.

Most upper-secondary students take English and mathematics, taken by 77 per cent and 71 per cent respectively of S5 and S6 students in 1993. The next most popular subjects were business subjects (29 per cent of students), biology (27 per cent), art and design (24 per cent), chemistry and physics (each 23 per cent) and computing subjects (21 per cent) (Scottish Office 1995: 4). These figures do not include subjects such as physical education and guidance which are part of the timetable of most students, but not usually certificated.

Despite the flexibility of upper-secondary courses, students do not usually pick and mix at random. Most schools impose curricular guidelines, for instance requiring English and mathematics, or structure the option columns to promote a coherent spread of subjects. NC modules are sometimes delivered in coherent clusters of three, and several local authorities have devised larger group awards. In 1992 General Scottish Vocational Qualifications (GSVQs), broad-based programmes of 12 or 18 NC modules, were introduced on a pilot basis. Like many other innovations in Scottish education, GSVQs responded to an English agenda (to be comparable to GNVQs) and are less appropriate for Scottish circumstances. In the absence of English-style tracks they do not have a large constituency within schools (Murray 1996). The kinds of students who take GNVQs in England attempt one or two Highers along with NC modules in Scotland; they are unlikely to sacrifice the currency of the Higher for a new award of uncertain status.

THE CASE FOR CHANGE

Towards the end of the 1980s upper-secondary-school courses came under increasing criticism. It was claimed that they lacked breadth and especially depth, and that the Higher represented a lower standard of attainment than the A level or its continental equivalents. Students were over-assessed, and the short Higher course – the 'two-term dash' – encouraged a teacher-centred pedagogy which left students ill prepared for more independent study in higher education. The system was failing to meet the needs of the more heterogeneous S5 population, especially middle-attaining students for whom Highers were too difficult but NC modules lacked coherence or status (Raffe 1997).

Many critics argued that Highers courses should be extended to two years. However, this was opposed by many Scottish educationists, who argued that a two-year Higher would reduce flexibility and access, and discourage participation since students staying on would have to commit themselves for two years. They also feared that it would imperil the four-year Scottish honours degree, which was symbolically linked to the fifth-year exit point from school. In 1990 the government appointed a committee under Professor John Howie to review courses and assessment in S5 and S6. Many people perceived that it had been appointed to introduce a two-year Higher, and much of the evidence submitted to the committee was conservative in tone, arguing that key features of the present system – including the flexibility of courses, the incremental course structure and the S5 exit point – should be preserved (McPherson 1992).

The committee's report was more radical (Scottish Office Education Department 1992). It endorsed the criticisms of the system that had been expressed and added some of its own – notably that there was an 'uneven gradient of attainment' which was too shallow in S1 and S2 and much too steep in S5, when many students found Highers difficult even after a Credit pass at Standard Grade in S4. The report argued that the S5 curriculum lacked coherence and that failure rates were too high, especially among middle-ability students taking one or two Highers. It proposed to advance Standard Grade to S3 and to introduce a twin-track system from S4 onwards. About 35-40 per cent of each cohort would follow a three-year programme, modelled on the academic track of Danish upper-secondary education; the others would follow a one- or two-year modular programme based on GSVQs.

The Howie Report punctured the complacency which had suffocated Scottish educational debate. It encouraged Scots to judge their system by European standards rather than through comparisons with England. Howie's diagnosis of the weaknesses of the current Scottish system was widely accepted, and Scotland is now almost unique among European education systems in having a consensus on the need to reform its leading qualification. There is no Scottish equivalent of the A-level lobby which has stifled change in England. However, the public consultations following the Howie Report revealed another point of consensus: that whatever the merits of Howie's diagnosis, his proposed remedy, the introduction of tracking into Scottish secondary schools, was unacceptable. Howie's twin-track system was almost universally rejected as divisive, impractical and in conflict with the Scottish comprehensive tradition (Howieson *et al.* 1997).

HIGHER STILL

The government took note of these reactions, and in March 1994 published *Higher Still: Opportunity for All* (Scottish Office 1994). This took Howie's diagnosis as its starting point but rejected his remedy. Instead it announced that a 'unified curriculum and assessment system' would be introduced, to cover all academic and vocational education beyond S4 and below the level of higher education. Scheduled for implementation in 1999, the system will embrace most FE and much adult provision as well as the upper-secondary school. The main exception is work-based provision, which will continue to be covered by Scottish Vocational Qualifications.

The main building blocks of the new system will be 160-hour courses. Each course is composed of three 40-hour units (or a 40-hour unit and an 80-hour unit) plus a further 40 hours 'for induction, extending the range of learning and teaching approaches, remediation, consolidation, integration and preparation for external assessment' (Higher Still Development Unit 1995). Units may also be studied and certificated separately. All courses and units, whether academic or vocational, follow consistent principles of curriculum design, assessment and certification. Units and courses will be available at five levels: Access, Intermediate 1, Intermediate 2, Higher and Advanced Higher. A student with a Credit pass at Standard Grade would normally progress to a Higher course in that subject in S5 (as at present); a student with a General pass would be likely to take that subject at Intermediate 2 level; and so on. Students may take a mixture of subjects at different levels, and may progress horizontally or vertically within the system. For example, S6 students who have passed Highers in S5 may choose to continue the same subjects at Advanced Higher or to take new subjects at Higher (or at a lower level if their prior attainment in the subject makes this advisable), or a mixture of the two.

The key to the Higher Still strategy is the single ladder of progression and attainment. Most education systems deal with the diversity of students by providing different ladders for students to climb, and allocating students to the ladder most suited to their climbing ability. This is what the Howie committee proposed for Scotland, with its twin-track model. Higher Still follows a different approach. It reorganises existing provision to form a single ladder, but allows students to start climbing at the rung on the ladder which corresponds to their prior level of attainment, and to climb at the speed which suits them. At the heart of this strategy is the introduction of rungs below Higher. A middle-attaining student with a General pass at Standard Grade, who in the past had to choose between a Higher which was too difficult or modules which lacked status, can now join the ladder at Intermediate 2 (the level below Higher) and remain in the educational mainstream, climbing to Higher and beyond in subsequent years. Hence the subtitle of *Higher Still: Opportunity for All*. However, the principle of the single ladder will be subverted if the system becomes a race: that is, if selectors in higher education or elsewhere only count attainments reached by a given age or stage such as the end of S6 (Raffe 1995).

The aims of Higher Still include the 'expansion and rationalisation of existing provision' and the 'consolidation of earlier reforms'. Most of the new units and courses are based on pre-existing provision. For example, most of the new Highers courses are developed from pre-existing Highers or from clusters of NC modules. Many courses below Higher level are based on NC modules. Some Advanced Higher courses are based on CSYS. Nevertheless, many courses and units have to be significantly modified in order to fit the new curriculum structure and to match the new principles of course design, assessment and certification. Some courses are being further revised in order to update the curriculum, to promote the integration of academic and vocational learning or to 'embed' core skills. Schools are being encouraged to treat Higher Still as an incremental process; initially they may offer only the courses and units which correspond to their current S5 provision, but as they become more familiar with the system they may feel able to offer the wider opportunities promised by Higher Still. Some of these wider opportunities may require collaboration among schools or between schools and colleges, and Higher Still could potentially transform the existing division of functions between schools and colleges.

Among the opportunities which many schools may only introduce after a few years are Scottish Group Awards. Based partly on GSVQs, each SGA defines a given level and breadth of attainment, including core skills, in a coherent subject grouping, and provides a basis for progression. 'Broadly based' SGAs are planned in five subject areas: arts and humanities, business and society, consumer studies, science and mathematics, and technological studies. 'Specialist' SGAs are planned in a large number of more vocationally specific fields; these are likely to be delivered mainly in FE (Higher Still Development Unit 1996). However, the specification of SGAs, including the distinction between broadly based and specialist SGAs, is currently under review. The future role and status of broad-based SGAs are a matter of speculation, and will depend among other things on the extent to which higher education recognises SGAs rather than their constituent courses as entrance qualifications.

Like other innovations in Scottish education, Higher Still is centrally led, with the Inspectorate playing an important role, and consultative. Two major consultation rounds in 1995 and 1996 gave educationists the opportunity to comment on proposals for courses and units as well as on more general issues such as assessment, certification, core skills and guidance. The Higher Still development has been billed as the largest consultation exercise in the history of Scottish education. The wide scope of the reform – introducing a unified system – makes a large-scale consultation both necessary and difficult. It makes it necessary because it aims to develop common principles and procedures throughout the diverse subjects, institutions and contexts of post-compulsory education in Scotland; this diversity must be represented in the consultation, so that all practitioners can raise issues which affect their specific situations. It makes it difficult because many practitioners cannot easily gain a perspective on the whole system of which their own practice forms a part. Consequently, although the consultation has been genuine, the role of consultees has been largely passive, responding to proposals rather than initiating them. The main outlines of the reform have not been changed by the consultation process. The reform process has just entered a new phase: in April 1997 the Scottish Examination Board and the Scottish Vocational Education Council, which used to award academic and vocational qualifications respectively, merged to form the Scottish Qualifications Authority, responsible for the new unified qualifications system.

The consultation has revealed wide support for the general aims of Higher Still, tinged with a degree of scepticism about the practicalities, including the time scale for reform, and anxieties over levels of resources and the effects on teacher workloads. Secondary education is suffering from innovation fatigue, an ageing workforce and a chronic and deteriorating shortage of resources. These are not the ideal conditions in which to implement a radical and visionary reform.

DISCUSSION: REFORM STRATEGIES FOR UPPER-SECONDARY EDUCATION

In Scotland as in other countries upper-secondary education faces the problems of expansion, both quantitative and qualitative. It must respond to new economic and social demands, and it must cater for students with a wider range of needs and abilities than the small and relatively homogeneous elite which it served a few decades ago. At the same time, it must respond to the rising aspirations of young people, who not only demand more education but are increasingly reluctant to pursue qualifications whose currency or status is lower than those of the academic mainstream. In nearly all countries, educational expansion is being fuelled by credentialism and by the drift into higher-status, academic courses (Pair forthcoming). In Scotland this has been reflected in the large number of students taking Highers and the failure of NC modules to establish a convincing alternative.

Countries have followed three main strategies in response to these pressures (Raffe 1993, 1996). Some, notably the German-speaking countries, have tried to resist the drift into academic courses by enhancing the status of their vocational tracks; this strategy emphasises the differences between the tracks so that vocational courses are not judged by the values of the academic track.

Most European countries, including England and Wales, are pursuing a second strategy, which retains tracks but seeks to develop closer links between them. Instead of emphasising the differences between tracks, this strategy emphasises the similarities. This may be done in various ways: by defining common levels of attainment across tracks, by introducing over-arching diplomas based on qualifications from either track, by introducing curricular elements such as core skills common to all tracks, or by facilitating transfer and mobility between tracks. The Dearing Report, on 16-19 qualifications in the United Kingdom except Scotland, exemplifies many of these approaches (Dearing 1996).

The third strategy is to develop a unified system, which avoids allocating students to groups but differentiates according to individual needs and abilities within a single framework of provision. Scotland is pursuing this strategy.

The first and second of these strategies presuppose the existence of clearly defined tracks in the first place. In Scotland there have been different courses (Highers and NC modules) but not different tracks, as most school students have combined the two. If the Scottish system was to be rationalised the choice was therefore between reintroducing tracking, as proposed by Howie, and a unified system.

Scotland has chosen a unified system. There are at least three possible reasons for this choice. The first is in order to realise a vision of the society of the future and of the role of education within it (Finegold *et al.* 1990; Young 1993). In this vision education transcends the division between academic and vocational learning with its arbitrary barriers to learning and progression; it serves the economy of the future, which requires new kinds of skills and knowledge and high levels of education for all the workforce; and it ends the social divisiveness of educational selection. However, Higher Still is not visionary, even by the standards of government documents. It presents the reform as a response to problems in the current system, as identified by Howie and others. Higher Still was informed by the more visionary ideas of unification, but these were not its main driving force.

The second reason is pragmatic. A unified system goes with the grain of Scottish upper-secondary education. The flexibility in the existing system and the absence of clear tracks make it easier to construct a unified system and relatively difficult to establish viable tracks. Scotland lacks a strong tradition of full-time vocational or technical education, and an attempt to develop a separate vocational track would founder on the strong pressures for academic drift within the system and on the preference of young people, employers and universities for academic rather than vocational qualifications. Had Howie's twin-track system been implemented, the upper track would have been massively oversubscribed, and the lower track would have had difficulty in establishing an identity (Raffe 1993).

The third reason is political. The Howie debate revealed a strong consensus in favour of a flexible course structure – not least among university interests, which associated it with the political argument for a four-year degree. The comprehensive school is more securely established, and has a stronger political base, than south of the Border; Howie-style tracking threatened the ethos, and perhaps also the institution, of the comprehensive school. The unified system also appeals to industry and to right-wing interests, because it raises the status of vocational education and its model of flexibility allows education to be responsive to employer demands (Howieson *et al.* 1997).

These factors influenced not only the choice of a unified system as the strategy for Scotland, but also the model of unified system which is being implemented. Higher Still emphasises flexibility and rationalisation; it eschews institutional reform such as the introduction of a Tertiary College; it leaves work-based provision untouched; its approach to curricular reform is cautious; and it will have relatively little impact on the university-bound student or on the academic ethos of Scottish education.

Hence the paradoxes with which I began. A reform which others perceive to be visionary and radical is presented within Scotland as an incremental change in keeping with educational and political conservatism. But all reforms, however radical, build on what already exists; reforms which do this consciously may be more likely to keep sight of their original aims (Fullan 1991). Higher Still has the potential to transform upper-secondary education in Scotland.

ACKNOWLEDGEMENTS

This chapter draws on the work of two research projects. The Unified Learning Project, funded by the Economic and Social Research Council (L 123 25 1039) as part of its programme on The Learning Society, is conducted jointly by the University of Edinburgh and the Post 16 Centre of the University of London Institute of Education. The project on Reforming Upper Secondary Education in Europe, supported by the European Commission as part of the Leonardo da Vinci Programme, is conducted by research teams in eight countries and is coordinated by the University of Jyväskylä. I am grateful to colleagues working on both projects, and especially to Cathy Howieson, Ken Spours and Michael Young, for help and support.

REFERENCES

Croxford, L., Howieson, C. and Raffe, D. (1991) 'National Certificate modules in the S5 curriculum', *Scottish Educational Review* 23(2): 78–92.
Dearing, Sir Ron (1996) *Review of Qualifications for 16–19 Year Olds*, London: SCAA Publications.
Finegold, D., Keep, E., Miliband, D., Raffe, D., Spours, K. and Young, M. (1990) *A British Baccalauréat? Ending the Division between Education and Training*, London: IPPR.
Fullan, M. (1991) *The New Meaning of Educational Change*, London: Cassell.
Higher Still Development Unit (1995) *The Frameworks of Units, Courses and National Certificates*, Consultation Document, Edinburgh: SCCC.
—— (1996) *Scottish Group Awards*, Consultation Document, Edinburgh: SCCC.

Howieson, C., Paterson, L., Spours, K. and Young, M. (1997) 'The state of the debates in England and Scotland on unifying academic and vocational learning', *Journal of Education and Work* 10(1): 5–35.

Lynn, P. (1996) *The 1994 Leavers*, Edinburgh: SOEID.

McPherson, A. (1984) 'Post-compulsory schooling: the sixth year', in D. Raffe, (ed.) *Fourteen to Eighteen*, Aberdeen: Aberdeen University Press.

—— (1992) 'The Howie committee on post-compulsory schooling', in L. Paterson and D. McCrone (eds) *The Scottish Government Yearbook 1992*, Edinburgh: Unit for the Study of Government in Scotland.

Murray, J. (1996) 'General Scottish Vocational Qualifications (GSVQs) in relation to the six themes of the post-16 strategies', in J. Lasonen (ed.) *Reforming Upper Secondary Education in Europe*, Publication Series B, Institute for Educational Research, University of Jyväskylä, Finland.

Pair, C. (ed.) (forthcoming) *Pathways and Participation in Vocational and Technical Education and Training* (provisional title), Paris: OECD.

Paterson, L. and Raffe, D. (1995) ' "Staying-on" in full-time education in Scotland, 1985-1991', *Oxford Review of Education* 21(1): 3–23.

Raffe, D. (1993) 'Multi-track and unified systems of post-compulsory education and "Upper Secondary Education in Scotland": an analysis of two debates', *British Journal of Educational Studies* 41(3): 223–52.

—— (1995) *One System at 16+ Years*, Briefing No. 3, Aiming for a College Education Scotland, Poole: BP International.

—— (1996) 'European strategies for parity of esteem', in J. Lasonen (ed.) *Reforming Upper Secondary Education in Europe*, Publication Series B, Institute for Educational Research, University of Jyväskylä, Finland.

—— (1997) 'The Scottish experience of reform: from Action Plan to Higher Still', in A. Hodgson and K. Spours (eds) *Dearing and Beyond: 14–19 Qualifications, Frameworks and Systems*, London: Kogan Page.

Scottish Education Department (1983) *16–18s in Scotland: An Action Plan*, Edinburgh: SED.

Scottish Office Education Department (1992) *Upper Secondary Education in Scotland* (the Howie Report), Edinburgh: HMSO.

Scottish Office (1994) *Higher Still: Opportunity for All*, Edinburgh: HMSO.

—— (1995) *The Curriculum in Education Authority Secondary Schools in Scotland 1989–1993*, Statistical Bulletin: Edn/C7/1995/8, Edinburgh: Government Statistical Service.

—— (1996) *Scottish School Leavers and their Qualifications: 1984–85 to 1994–95*, Statistical Bulletin: Edn/E2/1996/9, Edinburgh: Government Statistical Service.

Surridge, P. and Raffe, D. (1995) *The Participation of 16–19 Year Olds in Education and Training: Recent Trends*, CES Briefing No. 1, Edinburgh: Centre for Educational Sociology.

Weir, A. and Kidd, J. (1991) 'The National Certificate and Highers: a case of market forces', *Scottish Educational Review* 23(1): 13–22.

Young, M. (1993) 'A curriculum for the 21st Century? Towards a new basis for overcoming academic/vocational divisions', *British Journal of Educational Studies* 41(3): 203–22.

6

SPECIAL EDUCATIONAL PROVISION

Alison Closs

INTRODUCTION

All children in Scotland are entitled to free school education. Since 1974 *no* child has been deemed 'ineducable' or 'untrainable', however profoundly disabled. Where necessary, the cost of transport to school and subsistence expenses are also paid. Although special educational provision has been developed mainly for children with physical or sensory disabilities and/or cognitive learning difficulties, a significant change in the 1980s and 1990s is the recognition that children such as those with social and emotional difficulties, the very able and bilingual children may also experience difficulties in learning.

The following aspects are fundamental to special educational provision wherever it is located:

- expert advice from trained professionals,
- specialist approaches and resources,
- physically and emotionally adapted environments,
- multi-professional working,
- partnership with parents, and
- optimum involvement of the child.

HISTORICAL BACKGROUND

The development of special educational provision from its charitable foundations in the eighteenth century until the mid 1970s is recorded fully elsewhere (Petrie 1978). By the mid 1970s there were significant numbers of special schools, especially in the more densely populated central belt of Scotland, catering for the needs of officially identified 'categories' of handicapped pupils.

In Scotland such children were: blind, partially sighted, deaf, partially deaf, educationally sub-normal, epileptic, maladjusted, physically handicapped and those with speech defects.

Education authorities in the more sparsely populated rural areas to the south and north relied more on local school provision, in special units or classes or supported in ordinary classes. Reasons for this included: difficulties in transporting these pupils over long distances, financial non-viability of provision for small numbers of pupils within any category, and the willingness of local schools to support children in their own community. Such practice was in alignment with the 1955 Scottish Office Regulations, Circular 300, which advised authorities that:

> special educational treatment should be regarded simply as a well-defined arrangement within the ordinary educational system to provide for the handicapped child the individual attention that he particularly needs.
>
> (para. 4)

However, children with more severe disabilities often lacked regular specialist help, and some were sent away to residential special schools.

The year 1978 saw the publication of the Warnock Report (DES 1978), reporting the findings of a committee reviewing educational provision across Britain for 'handicapped' children and young people, and the specifically Scottish *Progress Report* (SED 1978) on the unsatisfactory 'remedial education' of children with learning difficulties in mainstream. The former was most influential in Scotland in promoting:

- the de-categorisation of children in favour of recognising and planning to meet their 'special educational needs',
- more provision for under-fives and over-sixteens,
- revision and expansion of specialist teacher training, and
- partnership between professionals and parents.

The latter proposed that:

- the curriculum be differentiated more effectively to meet the needs of *all* pupils on an individual basis,
- 'remedial' teachers become 'learning support' teachers, working with both pupils and teachers, and

- the mode and location of such help should mainly be collaborative teaching alongside class/subject teachers in the classroom.

Despite de-categorisation, some forms of description were retained for documentary, statistical, planning and research purposes. Annual data returns from special schools on all pupils and from mainstream schools on pupils with Records of Needs (see next section) now use the following headings:

hearing impairment	visual impairment
physical or motor impairments	language and communication
social and emotional difficulties	disorders
severe learning difficulties	moderate learning difficulties
specific learning difficulties	profound learning difficulties
other than the above	complex or multiple impairments

There are four sub-headings under 'complex or multiple impairments':

dual sensory impairment	moderate learning difficulties
severe learning difficulties	and other
and other	profound learning difficulties
	and other

LEGISLATION AND RESPONSIBILITY FOR SPECIAL EDUCATIONAL PROVISION

Special educational provision is subject to Scottish Office control and specifically Scottish legislation. Much responsibility is, however, devolved to the local education authorities, which have a duty to provide 'adequate and efficient' school education, including special educational provision, and to publicise the importance of early identification of children who may need such provision and opportunities for their assessment. The 1980 Education (Scotland) Act, as amended, is the current legal framework within which all special educational provision functions. Further guidance to the legislation is offered by two sets of Regulations, both 1982.

The law requires that special provision should be made for children who have greater difficulty in learning than their peers or who have a disability which impedes their use of the normal range of provision. Pupils between the ages of 2 and 19 are included, with school attendance mandatory for the 5–16 age group. Authorities may also assess, record and make provision for under-twos. Scottish Office Circular 4/96 offers a working definition:

> as a rule of thumb, it should be assumed that children or young people have a 'learning difficulty' if additional arrangements need to be made to enable them properly to access the curriculum.

(para. 9.2)

The 1980 Act also requires authorities to identify children and young persons who have 'pronounced, specific or complex special educational needs' which require continuing review, and to open and keep a Record of Needs for them. The Record, equivalent to the Statement of Needs in England and Wales, specifies the nature of a child's learning difficulties and the associated special educational needs, names a school and outlines the support which the authority intends to make. It is a legally binding document requiring multi-professional assessments of the child and the inclusion of parental views. Scottish Office Circular 4/96 indicates that the Record is intended to bring more method and stability to the planning and provision of education for such children.

Recording has been problematic in practice (Thomson *et al.* 1996), with its misuse in obtaining additional resources for individual children and schools, variable recording practices by and within authorities, lack of meaningful precision of the measures to be taken by the authority, and some ignorance on the part of parents of its purpose and their rights in relation to it.

Appeals about recording and placement and complaints about the efficacy of special educational provision are addressed by the Sheriff Court or by HMIs acting on behalf of the Secretary of State for Scotland, not by a special needs tribunal as in England and Wales. There is no specified time schedule for procedures in Scotland, unlike in England and Wales (DfE 1994). Parents have had less recourse to law than in England, but some individual and voluntary organisation-led cases against authorities have been successful. Authorities maintain that Scottish Office empowerment of parents of individual children, through legislation and publications (SOED 1993 and Kerr *et al.* 1994), has been at the expense of local authority policies and budgets designed to meet the needs of all.

A more consensual approach is now being adopted by the Scottish Office and local authorities, with authorities seeking to manage their budgets and meet their legal obligations by working cooperatively and openly with schools, parents and voluntary organisations. The entitlement of certain children to a Record as specified earlier must be met. However, the Scottish Office and authorities hope that the introduction of individualised educational programmes, 'IEPs', may help schools plan 'adequate and efficient education' for children with special educational needs, thereby reducing the demand for Records and additional resources for children.

LOCATION OF PUPILS WITH SPECIAL EDUCATIONAL NEEDS

(The data in this section come from the Scottish Office Statistical Bulletin on Provision for Pupils with Special Educational Needs, 1994 and 1995.)

Special educational provision may take place in mainstream classes, units within ordinary schools, special schools or other locations. Most regional authorities now provide the following within mainstream schools:

- special resource/support units,
- learning support teachers for pupils with learning difficulties,
- specialist peripatetic support services for maladjusted pupils and for those with physical and sensory impairments.

Support units act as full-time educational provision for some pupils and allow others to spend time both in the unit and in 'mainstream' classes, as appropriate to their needs. Support staff may work in special and/or mainstream contexts.

There has been a small reduction in the number of special schools. Independent and Scottish Office grant-aided special schools also provide education, in particular for children with sensory impairments, complex physical disabilities, and social, emotional and behavioural difficulties. Many such schools are residential, although frequent visits home are now routine. In response to pressure from parents and social workers in the late 1980s and early 1990s, some authorities have reduced residential placements and increased day provision. Fees are paid by the authority of the child concerned.

The 'care in the community' policies of the 1980s transferred children with complex and profound learning difficulties who had been placed in specialised and sometimes remote institutions back to their own or foster or adoptive families, who receive additional financial and practical help, or to more normal family-type care settings. They attend local special or ordinary schools with support. Most institutional special schools have been closed.

The small increase in integration in the early 1990s, mainly of children with sensory and physical disabilities, has not been sustained. Some parents have requested more specialist provision at the same time as other groups have demanded full inclusion. However, section 23 of the impending Children (Scotland) Act will give children 'affected by disability' the right 'to lead lives which are as normal as possible'. This may favour more inclusive models of education. A total of 1.2 per cent of all school pupils are currently being educated in special schools, this figure showing little change over the years, with 1.31 and 1.15 per cent respectively in 1950 and 1975. There has, however, been an 8 per cent increase in *real* numbers of special-school pupils between 1993 and 1995, and some special schools, especially those which cater for children with learning and behavioural difficulties, have waiting lists.

The oft-quoted phrase 'a continuum of provision to meet a continuum of need' suggests that there is a fitting placement for all children with special needs. The reality is sometimes less satisfactory for individual children, but authorities in the 1990s do try to ensure flexible use of existing facilities and services in the special and mainstream sectors to allow for parental choice and professional discretion. While some special schools still cater primarily for children with specific impairments, this is no longer assumed. This, and the legal right given to parents of *all* children in 1981 to request, within certain limits, that their child attend a certain school, has brought about a more varied population of children with special needs in both mainstream and special schools (Allan *et al.* 1995).

There are 201 special schools in Scotland, catering for over 9,000 pupils, comprising:

- 164 education authority,

- 7 grant-aided, and
- 30 independent schools.

A further 1,200+ pupils have most or all of their education in special units attached to primary (700 pupils) and secondary schools (500 pupils). There are over 14,000 pupils with Records of Needs, of whom over a third (2,642 in primary and 2,541 in secondary) spend *all* their time in mainstream classes. The number of recorded pupils has increased by 25 per cent since 1993, largely accounted for by an increase in demand for recording of pupils already enrolled in mainstream schools, rather than by any real change in school populations.

Examination of the data in relation to education authority special-school pupils and pupils with Records of Needs in primary and secondary schools, listed according to their impairments and their placements, indicates the following issues:

- pupils with moderate learning difficulties, with or without other difficulties, are the most numerous (42 per cent of the special-school population, 34 and 44 per cent of recorded primary- and secondary-school pupils respectively),
- the 1,150 recorded pupils with social, emotional and behavioural difficulties in mainstream schools are only the tip of an iceberg,
- the increase in numbers of recorded pupils with moderate learning difficulties and with social, emotional and behavioural difficulties in secondary, as compared to primary, may indicate difficulties specific to the secondary sector for such pupils and their teachers,
- the presence of over 700 pupils with severe, profound and/or complex learning difficulties in mainstream schools seems to indicate a trend towards inclusion, although most such pupils receive much or all of their education within special units, and
- the smaller number of pupils with language and communication difficulties in secondary schools possibly reflects less special unit provision at this stage, but may indicate successful early intervention enabling some pupils to return to mainstream.

The absence of data on the numbers of non-recorded pupils in mainstream schools who receive learning support of various kinds leaves a substantial area of provision unspecified.

CURRICULAR ARRANGEMENTS TO MEET SPECIAL EDUCATIONAL NEEDS

It is important to note that as far as possible pupils with special educational needs are included within the national curricular frameworks and guidelines for *all* pupils with only such alterations as are strictly in any child's educational interests. Many special schools are 'all-age' schools, sometimes taking pupils from age 3 to 19. Such schools do, however, generally differentiate primary from secondary sectors by moving from a single class teacher, with occasional special-subject teacher in-put, in primary to a more subject-specialist approach in secondary. The primary approach of a class teacher, often working with one or more auxiliaries, may, however, continue for the secondary age group in provision catering for the needs of pupils with more severe and profound learning difficulties, although age- and stage-appropriate approaches are advocated by SOEID.

Smaller SOEID-recommended class sizes in special schools give pupil–teacher ratios as follows:

- moderate learning difficulties 10:1,
- severe learning difficulties and physical disabilities 8:1,
- visual and hearing impairments, communication and language difficulties and social, emotional and behavioural difficulties 6:1.

More dependent groups of children also have auxiliary and/or nursery nurse support. For pupils with profound and complex learning difficulties the recommendation is that there should be a pupil–adult ratio of 5:2 and a pupil–teacher ratio of 10:1. Such recommendations are currently difficult to implement in the context of more heterogeneous special-school populations. Curricular support for individual pupils in mainstream is generally provided by a learning-support teacher working for short periods of time with the class or subject teacher, and in some cases practical help is also given by an auxiliary.

Despite such arrangements there are problems in delivering a broad and balanced curriculum, particularly in secondary departments of small, all-age, all-abilities schools. Foreign languages and individual sciences may not be taught in some schools. Such difficulties are addressed by the use of part-time staff and links with other special or mainstream schools or colleges, and by teachers extending their own subject and differentiation skills.

Pre-school special educational provision

Both special and mainstream provision is made. Some authorities give priority in nursery schools to children with special needs. Private, community-funded and voluntary organisation groups also make provision. Peripatetic specialist teachers may also work in children's own homes or with small groups. Their priority is helping parents to relate happily and developmentally to their children. There are good links between these services and the paediatric health services, from which many referrals come, often shortly after birth.

Primary-stage special educational provision

Special and mainstream provision has been well served, albeit rather belatedly, by the 5–14 curricular guidelines which build on existing good special educational practice. The flexibility of the guidelines, and assessment procedures provides an appropriate and clearly understood structure for the development of *all* children. However, abler pupils have needed extension beyond level E, and pupils with more severe learning difficulties have required more basic and detailed provision 'working towards level A'. Some pupils may actually spend their school career without achieving level A. Such appended developments might have been unnecessary had special needs professionals been included earlier in the planning process.

Subsequent development work by SCCC, with its positive history of curriculum development and publications in special educational needs, resulted in the publication of *Support for Learning* (SCCC 1992 and 1993), which offers general and specific guidance on how teachers should adapt, elaborate and extend the guidelines to meet the needs of pupils with special educational needs while remaining true to the guidelines' principles.

Secondary-stage special educational provision

Special schools may continue to implement the 5–14 guidelines up to and, more rarely, beyond the age of fourteen if appropriate.

However, they have not yet been fully implemented in mainstream schools, seriously disadvantaging some pupils with difficulties in learning. Increased levels of referral to special schools and requests for pupils to be recorded in S1 and S2 reflect inappropriate curricula, inability to cope with the demands of new subjects and many teachers, and a shortage of learning-support staff.

Disadvantage continues for the same pupils in S3 and S4 in schools which require all pupils to follow rigid 6–8 Standard Grade courses. Schools which offer a more supportive approach for a smaller number of courses have found that achievement is possible for some such pupils. More than 1,400 pupil-Standard Grade courses were undertaken in 1995 by special-school pupils, including those with learning and behavioural difficulties.

At this stage some special and mainstream schools have also made extensive use of SCOTVEC National Certificate modules and Skillstart awards developed specifically for students who had more difficulty in learning. Nearly 4,200 modules were undertaken by special-school pupils in 1995.

TVEI and the National Certificate provided an inclusively orientated foundation for the Higher Still Development Programme. This is revising and integrating the previous dual academic and vocational systems which bridge upper-secondary and further education for the sixteen plus population. Higher Still is the first curricular development which has offered 'opportunity for all' from its inception, by its creation of a special educational needs specialist group to guide developments and a team of development officers to work in all subject areas.

Further education colleges

Many young people with special educational needs now progress to college. Such provision was the single largest development in Scotland arising from the recommendations of the Warnock Report. All colleges in Scotland are required by the Further and Higher Education (Scotland) Act 1992 to consider the needs of students with disabilities and learning difficulties, and are funded to make both mainstream and special provision for them by the Scottish Office.

ROLES AND TRAINING OF KEY PROFESSIONALS

Multi-professional working underpins much special educational provision. Social work and paediatric health services are involved in the care and supervision of children with social, emotional and behavioural difficulties and of those with health problems respectively. Community-based paramedical services, including occupational, speech and language therapists and physiotherapists, work in special educational provision. While there is much excellent cooperative work there are also inherent stresses, related to shortage of time and personnel, changing personnel and differing professional perspectives. The full enactment of the Children (Scotland) Act in 1997 will make collaboration on behalf of 'children in need', including those with special educational needs, a requirement. Two successful areas of collaboration have been between social work and education personnel working with children and young people with social, emotional and behavioural difficulties in local Youth Strategy groups set up to establish better support for such children in their own communities, and between teachers and speech and language therapists working with communication-impaired children in schools.

Those most involved in special educational provision, however, are:

- educational psychologists,
- auxiliaries and nursery nurses,
- teachers, and
- advisers.

The provision of child guidance services, staffed by educational psychologists with a remit to study children who required special educational treatment, advise teachers and parents and make special educational provision, was begun in 1945 and made mandatory in 1969. Educational psychologists are particularly involved in the assessment of children with more pronounced difficulties and in supporting their teachers and parents. In many authorities they also have the main responsibility for dealing with recording and placement requests for children with special educational needs.

The training of educational psychologists takes two years of full-time study and practice following an honours degree in psychology. Some psychologists also have a teaching qualification, but this is not a requirement. Strathclyde and Dundee Universities offer this training, commencing courses in alternate years with 10–12 psychologists graduating each year. There were, in October 1996, 240 TFE educational psychologists in Scotland, which is insufficient to meet national demands. Although the professional target is of one psychologist to every 3,000 children, most authorities are functioning at a ratio of 1:4,500 or 1:5,000.

School and classroom auxiliaries make up more than 25 per cent of staff in special educational provision in mainstream and special schools – 3,000 full- and part-time staff in 1995. They provide practical and emotional support for children in and out of the classroom and most have received little or no formal training, relying on learning by experience. Training funds are now belatedly available for these staff, with courses in further and higher education establishments, some of them leading to SCOTVEC awards. Nursery nurses employed to work with younger children with special needs have a compulsory special needs element in their two-year National Certificate course.

The roles of teachers include assessing the strengths and needs of pupils, planning individualised educational programmes, direct teaching of individuals, groups and classes, managing pupils' progress and behaviour, offering personal guidance and counselling, liaising with other professionals and agencies involved, and reporting to and working cooperatively with parents, to name only some of the key activities.

Scottish teachers who undertake specialist training to work with such pupils must already be qualified primary or secondary teachers. In 1993 the Scottish Office produced competence-based guidelines for initial teacher training which required new teachers to be able to 'identify and respond appropriately to pupils with special educational needs or with learning difficulties'. Although training establishments have increased their input to undergraduates, it seems doubtful that all new teachers achieve this competence fully.

There is no legal requirement in Scotland for teachers working with pupils with special needs to have a specialist qualification, although many authorities, schools and parents prefer this. In 1992 just over half the teachers working in special educational provision had *no* specialist qualification, an unsatisfactory situation which some schools consider should be addressed by an enquiry equivalent to that recently conducted in England and Wales (DfEE 1996).

Specialist teacher award-bearing courses, available at the five main teacher education establishments, are now included as pathways within the Scottish postgraduate modular master's-level programme, with a four-module certificate and an eight-module diploma – generally accepted as a 'specialist teacher' award – followed by a four-module-equivalent research dissertation for a master's degree. A combination of core and option modules allows the full range of specialisms to be covered or a more generic approach for those in mainstream learning support or in management. This more academic model of training, dating from the early 1990s and delivered on a part-time evenings and weekends basis, represents the following significant changes from the previous model of a full-time one-year secondment course:

- there are fewer opportunities for teachers to experience working in other schools,
- exit is possible after four modules rather than eight, raising issues about width and depth of training,
- modules may be delivered on an 'outreach' basis in teachers' home areas and by open learning,
- there are stronger links to research, and
- more teachers, including non-specialist primary and secondary teachers, may access training because of reduced costs to employers, and less need for cover.

While the first two features are retrograde, the last, in view of the numbers of pupils with special needs in mainstream schools, is particularly desirable.

These research links in specialist training may promote needed further study of classroom experience and pupils' views in special educational research, already strong in Scotland. Higher education also hosts a range of specialist national centres and networks such as the Specific Learning Difficulties and Scottish Sensory Centres at Moray House and the Scottish Network for Abler Pupils at St Andrew's College.

Training leading to qualifications for teachers and auxiliaries is funded largely through a specific training grant from the Scottish Office to education authorities which may then devolve partly or wholly to schools, although many course members are also self-funding. Award-bearing courses at National Certificate and postgraduate master's levels, not eligible for the specific training grant, have also been developed for teachers and tutors working with students with special educational needs in further and community education.

Authority advisers and schools organise non-qualification in-service training in special needs. Much excellent special educational provision in Scotland has been developed by local-authority specialist advisers working with teachers. With the reorganisation in 1996 of local authorities into more and smaller single-tier authorities there is serious concern about the reduction and dispersal of such specialists, who also have a quality assurance role.

QUALITY ASSURANCE IN SPECIAL EDUCATIONAL PROVISION

Quality assurance in special educational provision is addressed nationally through HMIs, locally where the main legal responsibilities lie with authorities' officers and advisers, and increasingly by individual school managers. Performance criteria for learning support both for mainstream primary and secondary schools, for special educational provision wherever located, and for school ethos are in widespread use.

The publication of the report *Effective Provision for Special Educational Needs* (HMI 1994) describes approved school-based processes in planning, delivering and securing effective education for such children. A further publication, *A Manual of Essentials of Good Practice*, is in preparation. Inspectors' reports on individual schools and services are published, as well as reports on specific aspects of provision on a national basis. The Scottish Office four-yearly summary reports from the Audit Unit indicate that most provision has at least 'greater strengths than weaknesses'. The greatest areas of concern lie in secondary mainstream provision, where the capacity of learning support teachers to fulfil all their supportive and developmental roles is insufficient.

Scotland's apparent satisfaction with comprehensive education and mixed ability teaching is at odds with the relatively large numbers of children with moderate learning difficulties and with social, emotional and behavioural difficulties who are placed in separate special provision. More setting by ability is currently advocated nationally under the banner of *Achievement for All* (HMI 1996). The climate of achievement, the persistent subject-centredness of some secondary teachers and the difficulties of teachers in achieving effective levels of differentiation (Simpson and Ure 1994) suggest that setting would be desirable. However, setting could cause disaffection in lower-set pupils, and some pupils with specific difficulties may be difficult to set appropriately. Pupils who have greater difficulty in learning also benefit from working with more able pupils.

Six further issues of concern in the mid 1990s in Scotland are listed below:

1 Children with social, emotional and behavioural difficulties have not been brought fully into special educational procedures such as assessment and recording, despite their vulnerability, significant numbers in special residential provision and rising rates of exclusion.
2 Although public concern about discipline and disruption in schools and exclusion of pupils has not had such a high profile in Scotland as in England, there is serious professional concern. Scottish Office-funded research on these matters is in progress.
3 Special needs assessment of bilingual pupils in a Scottish authority has recently been seriously criticised by the Commission for Racial Equality (1996). The findings have implications for all authorities since the small bilingual population of Scotland is widely spread.
4 There is a continuing 'grey area' between cognitive learning difficulties in children and familial socio-economic disadvantage, relatively high in Scotland, which has not been addressed satisfactorily.
5 Children who are absent from school because of health problems, and excludees, do not have a statutory right to educational services out of school as children in England and Wales do, although some authorities make provision voluntarily.
6 While there is widespread acknowledgement of the importance of parents and the need to empower them in their children's education, there is still room to improve the partnership, particularly in utilising parents' knowledge of their children. Parents of children with special educational needs should also be made aware of the heavy financial and other demands made

on authorities and schools to meet the educational needs of *all* children.

Despite such concerns, the very high quality of much special educational provision should be acknowledged. This is due in part to the close links among local-authority and other providers and their committed staff, the Scottish Office and its HMIs, teacher education establishments and the voluntary sector, including parent organisations, and also to the national culture of co-operation.

REFERENCES

Allan, J., Brown, S. and Riddell, S. (1995) *Special Educational Needs Provision in Mainstream and Special Schools in Scotland*, Stirling: University of Stirling.

Commission for Racial Equality (1996) *Special Educational Needs Assessment in Strathclyde: Report of a Formal Investigation*, London: CRE.

DES (1978) *Special Educational Needs: Report of the Committee of Enquiry into the Education of Handicapped Children and Young People, (the Warnock Report)*, London: HMSO.

DfE (1994) *Code of Practice on the Identification and Assessment of Special Educational Needs*, London: HMSO.

DfEE (1996) *Professional Development to Meet Special Needs: Report of a Working Party of the Special Educational Needs Training Consortium*, Stafford: SENTEC.

HMI (1994) *Effective Provision for Special Educational Needs*, Edinburgh: Scottish Office.

—— (1996) *Achievement for All*, Edinburgh: HMSO.

Kerr, L., Sutherland, L. and Wilson, J. (1994) *A Special Partnership: A Practical Guide for Named Persons and Parents of Children with Special Educational Needs*, Edinburgh: HMSO.

Petrie, D. (1978) 'Development of Special Education since 1950', in W. Dockrell, W. Dunn and A. Milne (eds) *Special Education in Scotland*, Edinburgh: SCRE.

SCCC (1992) and (1993) *Support for Learning, Parts 1, 2 & 3*, Dundee: SCCC.

Scottish Office (1995) Circular 300, Edinburgh: Scottish Office.

Scottish Office (1996) *Provision for Pupils with Special Educational Needs, 1994 and 1995*, Statistical Bulletin, Education Series, Edn/D2/1996/11, Edinburgh: Scottish Office.

SED (1978) *The Education of Pupils with Learning Difficulties in Primary and Secondary Schools in Scotland: A Progress Report*, Edinburgh: HMSO.

Simpson, M. and Ure, J. (1994) *Interchange 30: Studies of Differentiation Practices in Primary and Secondary Schools*, Edinburgh: SOEID.

SOED (1993) *A Parents' Guide to Special Educational Needs*, Edinburgh: HMSO.

SOEID (1996) *Circular 4/96, Children and Young Persons with Special Educational Needs: Assessment and Recording,* Edinburgh: Scottish Office.

Thomson, G., Stewart, M. and Ward, K. (1996) *Interchange 40: Criteria for Opening Records of Needs,* Edinburgh: Scottish Office.

7

THE TEACHING PROFESSION
Its qualifications and status
Margaret M. Clark

In this chapter the development of the General Teaching Council in Scotland and its contribution to the status of the teaching profession will be discussed. Recent developments in the education of teachers and the relationship of these to changes in the curriculum in Scottish schools will then be considered.

THE GENERAL TEACHING COUNCIL: ITS ROLE IN SCOTTISH EDUCATION

The establishment of GTC

For over thirty years there has been a General Teaching Council in Scotland. In the 1960s there was considerable disquiet and unrest in the teaching profession in Scotland.

- Teachers' salaries were low in comparison with those in other professions.
- There was a shortage of teachers, which was worsening.
- The teaching profession saw itself as undervalued, and morale was low.
- There was concern about lack of consistency of standards of teaching in the schools.

Teachers felt that little regard was paid to their views; that they had little control over their own affairs; and that decisions were taken elsewhere, often for reasons they thought unjustifiable.

These concerns led in 1961 to a one-week strike by Glasgow teachers, protesting at dilution of standards and low pay. This was the first strike in the 114 years' history of the Educational Institute

of Scotland (the largest teachers' union in Scotland). The Secretary
of State for Scotland responded to these expressions of concern by
setting up a committee to examine the arrangements for the award
and withdrawal of certificates of competence to teach. The
majority of the members of the Wheatley committee were
certificated teachers. On the committee were practising teachers,
office-bearers of the professional associations, officials of the
Scottish Education Department, and representatives of the
colleges of education, the education authorities and the Scottish
universities. The balance of membership reflected to some extent
the membership of the General Teaching Council which was to
emerge.

Two years later when the committee reported, its central
recommendation was that a General Teaching Council for
Scotland should be established similar in scope, power and
functions to the councils in other professions. This recommendation was accepted by the Secretary of State, and the Council was
formally established by the Teaching Council (Scotland) Act 1965.
It is thus a 'statutory body'.

The Council

The Council plays a major role in Scottish education. It regulates
entry to the profession and it has a powerful voice in the vetting of
initial training courses for teachers and is responsible for the
assessment of probationary teachers.

I was a lecturer in a college of education in Scotland at the time
GTC was established, and remember the controversy which
surrounded its formation; in particular, the suggestion that
ultimately registration might be required of college lecturers as
well as teachers. Many of the developments that seemed either
revolutionary or impossible at that time have come to pass over
the years.

The Council is widely representative of the educational community. There are forty-nine members of the Council, in three
categories, elected, appointed and nominated members, as
follows:

(a) There are 30 elected members, all of whom are registered
    teachers (11 from primary schools, 11 from secondary schools,

5 from the teacher education institutions and 3 from the further education sector.

(b) Fifteen non-elected members are appointed by the Scottish Higher Education Institutions, the Association of Directors of Education in Scotland, the Convention of Scottish Local Authorities and the churches.

(c) Four members are nominated by the Secretary of State for Scotland. These are usually parents, industrialists, accountants or solicitors chosen for their additional experience and expertise.

There are also two assessors appointed by the Scottish Office Education and Industry Department.

The following three points are important:

(a) GTC is a teaching council, not a teachers' council. In short, the Council created is widely representative of the educational community, not composed exclusively of teachers.

(b) Elected membership is on the basis of national elections. Nomination by teachers' unions was rejected by the Wheatley committee and again later on review.

(c) The Council is independent of the Scottish Office Education and Industry Department. The Council is not a government body; it does, however, work closely with the Department on matters of mutual concern.

Every teacher registered to teach in Scotland pays an annual registration fee. The Council receives no funding from outside sources. It is considered important that it is self-financing and is therefore independent.

The Council's main role is to maintain the quality of the profession. Threats to this may come from central government, local authorities, schools or departments within these or training institutions.

The Council protects professional standards by maintaining a register of qualified teachers, advising on the supply of teachers, overseeing standards of entry to the profession, accrediting and reviewing all courses of initial teacher education and exercising disciplinary powers in relation to registration.

The issue of partnership between teacher education institutions and schools in initial teacher education has been considered by a working group of the General Teaching Council. Its report, while stressing that the concept of partnership in initial teacher education is not new, states that a national framework is desirable to ensure a consistency of approach (GTC 1997).

Registration

The Council keeps a register of the names of those entitled to teach in public-sector schools in Scotland. In 1996 there were over 77,000 teachers on the register. It is illegal for an education authority to employ a teacher in a nursery, primary, special or secondary school who is not registered with the Council. Most private schools also prefer to employ registered teachers.

Staff in teacher education institutions concerned with the professional education of teachers must be registered. After a lengthy campaign this was achieved in 1986. The requirements for the registration of lecturers involved in teacher education are the same as those for primary and secondary teachers. All lecturers involved with the theory and practice of teaching are required to have primary or secondary registration, as appropriate, or in very limited numbers of cases, registration in further education.

Registration is not yet compulsory for further education teaching staff; however, the Council continues to press for this. There is no statutory requirement for educational psychologists to be registered. However, many education authorities in their job specification require that educational psychologists should be registered teachers. The General Teaching Council is seeking to establish a role in the post-probationary education of teachers.

Probation

The majority of teachers in Scotland have been trained in one of the Scottish teacher education institutions and are automatically eligible for admission to the register. Initially they have only provisional registration. They have to serve two years of 'probation' before they are admitted to full membership. At the end of the two years the probationer's headteacher indicates whether the probationer should be granted full registration, have provisional registration extended by a period of up to a year or have provisional registration withdrawn. Such action is taken where necessary, and each year a few probationers are removed from the register.

Since 1992, all graduates from teacher training institutions have received a copy of the updated pack 'Welcome to Teaching', which includes valuable training material and information. New training units for headteachers and those with responsibility for probationers have been issued to all schools and local authority centres in Scotland .

Teachers trained outside Scotland are the responsibility of a committee on exceptional admission. This area of the Council's work has increased significantly as a result of developments within the European Community. Approximately 900 applications for such registration were received in 1994.

Supply of teachers

The Council is one of the Secretary of State's formal advisers on the supply of teachers, a duty carried out in cooperation with colleagues in the local authorities and colleges of education. How important at any particular time is the role of the supply committee depends on whether there is an under- or over-supply of teachers.

Disciplinary powers

As will be appreciated by the fact that in Scotland teachers must be registered with GTC, withdrawal of registration is a powerful disciplinary power. A registered teacher who is found guilty of professional misconduct and whose name is removed from the register would no longer be entitled to teach in a school in the public sector in Scotland. The investigating and disciplinary committees contain a majority of serving teachers. Currently some members feel that there are not sufficient options open to these committees and that it would be helpful if powers were extended to include some forms of censure and suspension. While the Council at present has the power to investigate cases of teachers who are already registered and applicants for registration, it does not have the power to investigate students at the point of entry to training. Some may consider this a weakness in the present system.

Initial teacher education and GTC

There is an accreditation and review committee. This operates in two ways. All courses of initial teacher education must be acceptable to the General Teaching Council as leading to registration. Thus institutions must submit documentation relating to new courses for scrutiny. If a course is given unconditional approval it can proceed with five successive intakes of students before there is a major review. When a course is under review the views of current students, headteachers of schools which have provided school experience and, on occasion, probationers may be sought.

It is worthy of note that the Council is the Secretary of State's principal adviser on initial teacher education. In 1990 the Council was invited to undertake a survey of the one-year postgraduate primary course. The main recommendations of that report are now to be implemented. This shows a recognition of the Council's important role in the professional education of teachers.

GTC and the teaching profession

The existence of the General Teaching Council in Scotland has been important not only for the teaching profession but also for education in Scotland over a period which has seen many stresses placed on the profession. While teachers in Scotland have not entirely escaped these pressures, they have certainly been protected from some of them, and their professional status, even perhaps their morale, is probably higher than that of teachers south of the Border. There is an ample supply of well-qualified applicants for teacher training. Some courses, PGCE (Primary) for example, remain over-subscribed by a ratio of 8:1. The drop-out rate from training is low and the retention rate in the profession is high. The problem in Scotland currently is the large number of unemployed teachers. The Council has benefited the profession in the following ways:

1 Professional standards are seen to be protected. One of the first steps taken by the Council was the removal from the schools of unqualified persons. GTC also played an important role in making teaching an all-graduate profession.
2 The retention not only of a two-year probationary period for teachers in Scotland but also of further training during the two

103

years owes a great deal to GTC. Support materials designed to improve the quality of that experience have been developed by GTC.

3 Registration is now required by staff in teacher education institutions in Scotland; thus the Council has a role in promoting the continuing professional development of staff, and encouraging collaborative models between the colleges and schools.

4 GTC has an important role in ensuring the maintenance of professional standards in the wake of the EC Directive on greater freedom of professionals within the European Community.

To be the professional voice of the teaching profession a Council must be able to reflect the views of the whole profession. It must therefore have a wide base, be independent and be seen to be apolitical. Such a role is not possible for the unions, which are often political and do not always speak with one voice, something on which governments frequently capitalise.

In Scotland, as shown by government statistics, there is a nearly perfect match in secondary schools between qualifications and subjects taught, which is a long way from being achieved in some countries. In a Policy Review 1992–3 of the General Teaching Council for Scotland, the Scottish Office Education Department pays tribute to the Council's influence in achieving this:

This close match between the qualifications of Scottish teachers and the subjects they are required to teach stands in sharp contrast to the position in England and Wales where there is no equivalent of the General Teaching Council. . . . It must be recognised that, were there no such body, the retention of this level of control would be extremely difficult and standards in Scottish education would be at risk.

(SOED 1992: 9)

In Scotland GTC is consulted by government on major issues and employing authorities do pay regard to its policies. The report quoted above gives due recognition to the important role of GTC, and to its cost effectiveness. The Scottish Office report commends the Registrar and staff for the 'level of sophistication in their administrative control' (p. 13). With the range of duties for which the Council is responsible and the size of the register which it is required to maintain, clearly the administrative staff play a crucial role. I had personal experience of their efficiency and the speed with which they deal with enquiries when I prepared this chapter.

It is interesting to note in *Link* (GTC for Scotland Newsletter 21, winter 1995) that GTC is mounting a series of educational conferences under the title 'Towards the Millennium'. In the same publication there is an article by Patrick O'Neill, who was sent to Edinburgh from Ontario by his union to take a first-hand look at GTC. This was in anticipation of the establishment there of such a body, which he reports was viewed with scepticism and trepidation by the unions and professional associations. However, he comments that in Scotland he found that:

> the unions were just as happy with the achievements of the Council in terms of guarding the standards of the profession as were the individual teachers. The unions were particularly enthusiastic about the role of the Council in accrediting and reviewing teacher education programmes, and in being so fastidious in dealing with the probation period. . . . The success of the GTC has inspired teachers in many other parts of the world to think about and aspire to developing and putting in place a truly self-regulating profession. It remains to be seen if the success of Scotland can be equalled.
>
> (O'Neill 1995: 8)

O'Neill claims that the Scottish Education Department was likewise enthusiastic about the role and performance of the Council: it was suggested that if there were no Council, the work that it does would have to be done, most probably by the Department, and it was admitted that it would cost a lot more.

Reviews by the convenors of the various committees of GTC are to be found in the *Quadrennial Review* (GTC for Scotland 1995).

TEACHER EDUCATION

Teacher education institutions

According to the SOEID *Memorandum* on Teacher Education (SOEID 1996), there are now ten institutions in Scotland which provide courses of initial teacher education. The following six institutions offer a number of such courses:

1 The University of Paisley, whose Faculty of Education is the former Craigie College;
2 The University of Strathclyde, whose Faculty of Education is the former Jordanhill College;
3 Moray House Institute of Education, Holyrood Campus;
4 Northern College, Aberdeen Campus;
5 Northern College, Dundee Campus;
6 St Andrews College (Scotland's National Catholic College).

The following is a list of the courses available and the number of the above institutions where they run:

- Bachelor of Education Primary (B.Ed.) (all six);
- Bachelor of Education Secondary in Music (three) and in Technological Education (two);
- Postgraduate Certificate of Education (PGCE Primary) (five);
- PGCE Secondary (five);
- Combined degree (three).

(PGCE Primary is available only at the Dundee Campus of Northern College and PGCE Secondary only at the Aberdeen Campus.)

The following four institutions are listed as providing only one course:

7 The University of Glasgow, Robert Clark Centre for Technological Education offers a B.Ed. Secondary in Technological Education.
8 Moray House Institute of Education, Cramond Campus offers a B.Ed. Secondary in Physical Education.
9 The Scottish School of Further Education, Strathclyde University offers Further Education.
10 The University of Stirling offers combined degrees.

Entry requirements

The minimum entry requirements for admission to courses of teacher education in Scotland are determined by the Secretary of State for Scotland in consultation with the General Teaching Council for Scotland. Beyond these minimum requirements the decision on acceptability rests with the teacher education institutions. The 1996 *Memorandum* referred to above sets out the minimum requirements for the session 1997–8 and lists further requirements due to come into effect by 2000. Reference in the *Memorandum* is to the Scottish Certificate of Education and equivalent qualifications (responsibility for judging the latter rests with the teacher education institutions).

There are two alternative courses leading to the Teaching Qualification (Primary Education):

(a) A four-year course leading to a Bachelor of Education degree (B.Ed.), which has the following minimum requirements for entry – Higher Grade passes in at least three subjects, one of which must be English, and Standard Grade in two other subjects. Mathematics must be one of the subjects (and in 2000 a higher level of qualification in mathematics will be required).
(b) A one-year Postgraduate Certificate of Education (PGCE) course which follows the award of a degree. Additional requirements for English and mathematics which apply to the B.Ed. also apply. Teacher education institutions are also expected to consider the contents of the applicant's degree, ensuring that it provides the necessary foundation for work as a primary teacher.

There are three alternative routes to the Teaching Qualification (Secondary Education):

(a) a four-year course leading to a B.Ed. degree in music, physical education or technological education;
(b) a combined degree with subject study, study of education and school experience;
(c) a one-year Postgraduate Certificate of Education (PGCE).

An applicant's initial degree must contain specific subject study relevant to the intended teaching qualification and enable the applicant to teach the subject in Scottish secondary schools. There are specific requirements which applicants must meet for individual subjects.

It should be noted that the Teaching Qualification (Secondary) is awarded in a particular subject or subjects of the secondary school curriculum. It is possible to obtain a teaching qualification in more than one subject. There are also conversion courses for registered teachers which enable them to gain additional teaching qualifications, also provided at the teacher education institutions.

Successful completion of a course of teacher education at a Scottish teacher education institution leads to an award of a teaching qualification. However, as noted earlier, registration with GTC is a statutory prerequisite for employment as a teacher in education-authority primary, secondary, special and nursery schools in Scotland.

GUIDELINES FOR INITIAL TEACHER EDUCATION

General guidelines

Revised guidelines were issued in 1993, which were to apply to all new courses of initial training and those requiring revalidation (SOED 1993). By 1995–6 they were to apply to all courses. A working party reported on Primary Pre-service Training in 1983 and on Secondary Postgraduate Pre-service Training in 1985. The current guidelines are a revision and consolidation of those issued from 1983 onwards. The guidelines stress the role of the schools in which students gain their practical experience, partner schools, and what are referred to as competences in teaching. These professional competences do not refer only to practical skills, but also to knowledge and understanding both of the content of the teaching, and the relationship between the children's learning and the methods of teaching employed.

All courses must be validated by a university or degree-awarding institution; must be acceptable to the General Teaching Council; and must be planned to make use of the core competences set out in the Guidelines (SOED 1993). School experience must be jointly planned by the institution, schools and education authority. The orientation of the course must be professional, with performance in teaching being essential for a pass and the schools having a role in assessment.

The general competences listed are grouped under the following headings:

- competences relating to subject and content of teaching;
- competences relating to the classroom, which include: communication, methodology, class management, assessment;
- competences relating to the school;
- competences related to professionalism.

There are also specific conditions depending on the teaching qualification sought.

The Teaching Qualification (Primary Education)

- Courses must be designed to teach children of the 3–12 age range across the primary curriculum.
- Students must be given extended experience in the upper-middle and lower stages of the primary school and with children who have not yet entered Primary 1, in a nursery school or class.
- Particular attention must be paid to current national curricular developments, including the 5–14 Programme.
- The students' study of the primary curriculum must be linked closely to both professional studies and school experience.

The B.Ed. course leading to a primary qualification which lasts for four years may be offered at ordinary or honours level. School experience, which must be of not less than thirty weeks, must occur in each year of the course. In addition to the areas of the primary curriculum, students are required to study in depth two optional subjects; a modern language should be one of the available options. The PGCE (Primary) course is a full-time course of thirty-six weeks, of which at least 50 per cent is devoted to school experience, which will occur in each term.

The Teaching Qualification (Secondary Education)

The course must be designed to train teachers to teach pupils of the 12–18 age range in one or more subjects in an approved named subject. Some consideration is to be given to the needs of adults now taught in some secondary schools. The students' study of the secondary curriculum is to be closely linked to professional studies and school experience and, as for primary, to include current national curriculum developments. The course must contain an element of experience in the primary school.

The PGCE (Secondary) course is a full-time course lasting for 36 weeks, at least 22 weeks of which are devoted to school experience, with a block in each term. The B.Ed. (Secondary) is available in music, technology and physical education, each of which has special conditions laid down.

ASSESSMENT OF QUALITY OF TEACHER EDUCATION

Under the Further and Higher Education (Scotland) Act 1992 the Scottish Higher Education Funding Council (SHEFC) is required to undertake assessments of the quality of teaching and learning in higher education institutions. In teacher education, Her Majesty's Inspectors, who are the principal advisers to the Secretary of State for Scotland, have led the assessments with support from assessors seconded from higher education and local-authority education departments. During 1994–5, evaluations of the B.Ed., the PGCE primary and secondary courses and the combined degree at the University of Stirling were undertaken (SHEFC 1995). The publication is intended as a reference tool for the guidance of teachers and prospective students. Each institution was visited by 4–6 assessors, and the reports have similar headings: curriculum; environment and resources; teaching and assessment; school experience; student guidance and support; outcomes and quality control and conclusion. The conclusion indicates the particular strengths and areas in which improvements could be made and gives an overall judgement on the quality of teacher education.

The quality of teacher education at the following five institutions was judged as highly satisfactory: Moray House Institute of Education, the University of Paisley, St Andrew's College, the University of Stirling, Strathclyde University.

The remaining institution, Northern College (with a campus in Aberdeen and one in Dundee), was rated as satisfactory.

Figures are given for the number of staff involved in teacher education and the number of students on the various courses at each institution at the time of the assessment (1994–5). The total number of students on each course is as follows: B.Ed. 2,971, PGCE Primary 257, PGCE Secondary 1,215.

(The figures are not given for the University of Stirling which offers a combined degree for which students study education alongside other subjects which they take in other departments, leading to a degree plus a diploma, which qualifies them to teach in secondary schools.)

Thus the institutions in Scotland providing courses of initial teacher education were all rated as highly satisfactory or satisfactory, and as reflecting in their courses the 1993 *Guidelines for Teacher Training Courses* from the Scottish Office Education Department described in the previous section.

PARTNERSHIP WITH SCHOOLS IN TEACHER EDUCATION

In the United Kingdom, government policy on teacher education is becoming more precise as to what competences must be covered during inital teacher education. Schools are also being encouraged to take a more dominant role. The existence of the General Teaching Council has, however, limited the extent to which government can dictate the precise nature of courses in Scotland. The very presence of GTC does indicate an existing partnership between the teaching profession and the institutions of higher education involved in initial teacher education. In addition to specific competences for individual courses, current guidelines in Scotland for all courses lay stress on general competences to be covered during initial teacher education; that is, for teachers involved with pupils from 3 to 18 years of age. These include 'professional competences', including the importance of understanding and critical thinking. In Scotland, in contrast to England, so far at least, there has not been an attempt in the guidelines to lay down the methods of teaching to be employed in the classroom.

There is no suggestion in the guidelines for courses in Scotland that the schools should take the leading role in planning and providing courses; rather the thinking is that they should work in partnership with the institutions. There is some research evidence of the kind of partnership which exists in Scotland. Students' views on college/school partnership have been explored by Moray House College of Education. Preceding the publication of the guidelines referred to above, a national pilot study of the new arrangements took place with over 200 students on a PGCE Secondary course. This study showed that the students expected, and at the end of their course believed, that the schools had made greater impact on their professional development than the college. A sub-group given additional time with schools and teachers, with specially trained mentors, did better and felt happier about their course. It should be noted that this study was of students training as secondary teachers, not primary teachers – who would feel that they already had sufficient knowledge of their subject. When students qualify as teachers and apply for jobs, reports on their training in Scotland have a standard format. The comments on their performance in schools are highly regarded by prospective employers. Thus in Scotland schools are not seen as junior partners in teacher education either by the students or by prospective employers (see Cameron-Jones 1995).

As was noted earlier, the GTC examined what the most appropriate forms of partnership are and what they entail (GTC 1997). In an article in *The Times Educational Supplement* (Scotland), Gordon Kirk, Principal of Moray House Institute of Education, considers the benefits of collaboration to both the schools and the institutions. He stresses the distinctive contribution each can make and the benefits to the schools as well as to the higher education institution in partnership, and proposes that successful partnership appears to involve the sharing of power. He suggests the need for a formal mechanism through which the collaborative activities can be planned and evaluated. Finally, he stresses the need for appropriate resourcing of partnership initiatives; that they must not be seen merely as a way of providing teacher education on the cheap (Kirk 1996: 18).

IN-SERVICE AND PROFESSIONAL DEVELOPMENT FOR TEACHERS

There have been major developments in Scotland in post-experience courses for teachers since 1984. Prior to that, although colleges of education made a heavy investment of time and resources in practice-orientated in-service courses, there were no nationally integrated courses. Master of Education (M.Ed.) courses were offered by Scottish universities, often on a part-time basis for practising teachers. These award-bearing courses, seen by many teachers as important for promotion, for entry to posts in teacher education and universities, were predominantly theoretical in contrast to the courses offered by the colleges of education.

In 1984, the National Committee for the In-Service Training of Teachers (NCITT) set out a national strategy for in-service training based on three levels of award:

- Level 1 Certificate courses requiring one term's study or equivalent;

- Level 2 Diploma (or in-service B.Ed. degree courses to allow non-graduates to raise their qualifications) requiring the equivalent of three terms' study;
- Level 3 Master's degree, requiring the equivalent of four terms' study.

The programmes had the following characteristics: the levels were qualitatively different, many of the awards were based on national guidelines, the requirement for external validation and quality assurance through external assessment and evaluation met the need for accountability.

There were a number of tensions during the development of this programme, not least that changes in government funding for in-service training meant that the colleges found themselves in competition with the regional authorities and schools for staff development revenue.

The Scottish Credit Accumulation and Transfer (SCOTCAT) framework is the national credit framework relating to higher education in Scotland. In 1991 all higher education institutions joined together in establishing a common framework within which credit-based learning would be developed. The first edition of the *SCOTCAT Quality Assurance Handbook* has been developed after extensive consultation, and it is acknowledged there that further work is required to refine the concepts, and on international credit transfer (HEQC 1995).

During the 1990s, with most colleges of education either now part of universities or with closer links to them, the way has been open for further developments, while important features of the structure noted earlier have been retained. Institutional collaboration over planning the national guidelines has provided a basis from which a national scheme of credit accumulation and transfer within Scotland could be developed. The three-tier structure, with flexible modular schemes and credit transfer, provides teachers with the possibility of planning their programme to meet their needs and is an encouragement to continuing professional development. However, limitations in resources available for specialised training and further professional development place barriers in the way of initiatives such as these. This section is based mainly on 'In-service and professional development: the emergence of post-graduate award schemes' (Landon 1995).

ACKNOWLEDGEMENT

I wish to acknowledge the help I received with the section on the General Teaching Council from David I. M. Sutherland, the Registrar for GTC Scotland. In particular, I have leaned heavily on the text of a speech he delivered at a conference in Australia.

REFERENCES

Cameron-Jones, M. (1995) 'Permanence, policy and partnership in teacher education', in G. Kirk (ed.) *Moray House and Change in Higher Education*, Edinburgh: Scottish Academic Press.

GTC for Scotland (1995) *Quadrennial Review and Accounts 1991–95*, Edinburgh: GTC for Scotland.

—— (1997) *Report of the Working Group on Partnership in Initial Teacher Education*, Edinburgh: GTC for Scotland.

HEQC (1995) *The SCOTCAT Quality Assurance Handbook 1995*, London: HEQC and Glasgow: HEQC Glasgow Office.

Kirk, G. (1996) 'Who'd be a collaborator?', *Times Educational Supplement Scotland*, 11 October: 18.

Landon, J. (1995) 'In-service and professional development: the emergence of post-graduate award schemes', in J. O'Brien (ed.) *Current Changes and Challenges in European Teacher Education: Scotland*, Brussels: COMPARE–TE Network.

O'Neill, P. (1995) 'Congratulations Scotland', *Link* 21, Edinburgh: GTC for Scotland: 8.

SHEFC (1995) *Reports of a Quality Assessment in Teacher Education*, Edinburgh: SHEFC.

SOED (1992) *General Teaching Council for Scotland: Policy Review 1992–93*, Edinburgh: SOED.

—— (1993) *Guidelines for Teacher Training Courses*, Edinburgh: SOED.

SOEID (1996) *Memorandum on Entry Requirements to Courses of Teacher Education in Scotland*, Edinburgh: HMSO.

8

STANDARDS AND QUALITY

Pamela Munn

Scotland's approach to monitoring standards and improving quality in schools is based on the belief that 'the most effective way of improving the quality of education for individual pupils is to expect schools to take responsibility for their own quality assurance by evaluating their performance and making the necessary changes' (HMI 1996). This belief means that national standards are monitored in a variety of ways and the results disseminated to schools with the aim of encouraging schools to reflect upon and improve aspects of their own practice. As in many countries, a prime concern in Scotland is with pupils' attainments at various stages of their school careers. More unusual, perhaps, is a concern too with certain school processes which are seen as contributing to attainment. These include a positive school ethos, effective school development planning and, associated with these, consultative management styles.

This chapter is in three main parts. First, a brief summary of current sources of evidence about standards is given. Second, an overview of standards in primary and secondary schools is provided. Third, some examples of various initiatives designed to improve quality are described.

SOURCES OF EVIDENCE ABOUT STANDARDS AND QUALITY

There are several major sources of evidence. The first is HM Inspectorate's programme of independent inspection. There are about eighty HMIs, headed by a Senior Chief who is the professional adviser within education to the Secretary of State for Scotland. There is no OFSTED in Scotland. Within the

Inspectorate, there is an Audit Unit whose job it is to 'collect, analyse and publish evidence about how well schools and education authorities are performing' (SOED 1991).

The Unit intends to publish a report on standards and quality in Scottish education every three years; it recently published an overview for 1992–5. This report is, and no doubt successive reports will be, structured around published performance indicators from HMI. These fall under seven broad headings: the Curriculum, Standards of Attainment, Quality of Teaching and Learning, Support for Pupils, Ethos, Resources and Management and Quality Assurance (HMI 1996). The indicators relate judgements to four levels of performance:

- very good – major strengths
- good – strengths outweigh weaknesses
- fair – some important weaknesses
- unsatisfactory – major weaknesses

Inspectorate evidence is based on visits to schools and classrooms; lessons are observed, documents are analysed and a range of pupils, parents and staff interviewed. The 1992–5 report was based on inspections of 260 primary and 80 secondary schools, for which individual reports were published. In addition 'aspect inspections' are undertaken focusing on particular topics such as special educational needs provision or guidance. The report includes evidence based on these kinds of inspections and so includes evidence from the inspection of more than 9,000 primary-school classes and 12,000 secondary-school classes.

The second source of evidence about standards is the Assessment of Achievement Programme (AAP). This monitors pupils' attainments in English language, mathematics and science at stages P4, P7 and S2, by testing a sample of pupils in a range of schools. One of these subjects is tested every year and then again at three-yearly intervals. The results are published regularly and distributed in user-friendly summaries to all schools in Scotland. There are, at the time of writing, no performance tables of primary schools in Scotland. Plans to introduce these were resisted by parents and others in 1991–2 and an alternative system was introduced. This gives primacy to teacher assessment at a time the teacher thinks right for the individual pupil, and test results are private. There are therefore national tests in that there are test items, but there is no national testing when pupils sit tests across the country at the same time.

A third source is the annual publication of pupils' attainments in the national examinations Standard Grade, National Certificate and Higher at ages 16, 17 and 18. Standard tables of examination results developed by SOED have been provided by the Scottish Examination Board (SEB) each year since 1991. These tables provide actual results[1] and national comparison factors. National comparison factors allow direct comparison of school presentations and results with national averages. In addition, relative ratings provide information on a pupil's performance in a range of subjects within the same school. These tables have been accompanied by a support pack for schools on how to use the information on pupils' attainments (HMI 1991; 1993). They have also been accompanied by a range of criticisms of their validity and reliability as a measure of school effectiveness. (See, for example, Brown and Riddell 1992; McPherson 1992; Willms 1992.)

A fourth source has been a series of research studies undertaken in the former Scottish Regions, involving teachers, policy-makers and researchers working together to understand the strengths and limitations of indicators of school quality. A recent example is the study by Croxford and Cowie (1996) on the effectiveness of Grampian schools. This particular study reports a rise in average attainment in public examinations in 1992–4. It explains differences in average attainment among Grampian schools in terms of pupil intakes.

A fifth source is Scotland's participation in a number of comparative studies of pupil attainment. Scotland continues to participate in Organisation for Economic Cooperation and Development (OECD) studies and recently took part in the *Third International Mathematics and Science Study* (TIMSS), in which Scottish children's attainments were compared to those of children in a number of European, American and Australasian countries (SOEID 1996a).

Finally, local authorities have quality assurance units which undertake a programme of school review. They use similar, though not identical, performance indicators to HMI and are in a position to visit more schools more regularly.

---

1 Results at Higher Grade are used to measure the 'value-added' or boost to pupils' performance provided by the school.

STANDARDS IN PRIMARY SCHOOLS

The most extensive source of evidence is HMI. The 1992–5 report (HMI 1996) highlights the following:

- curriculum – all primary schools had a broad curriculum in line with the 5–14 Programme
- attainment – in over 70 per cent of schools most pupils exceeded or reached national targets in English language and mathematics. Areas signalled as weaknesses were aspects of writing, in particular the need to make greater use of extended writing and of redrafting. In mathematics there was some concern about problem-solving and enquiry. There was also concern about science and technology. (See the section on secondary education for more detail.)
- learning and teaching – quality was reported as good or very good in 85 per cent of schools. 'Most pupils were industrious, well motivated and responsive to their teachers.' There was concern about the failure of many schools to set homework beyond English language and mathematics.
- support for pupils – this was reported as very good or good in over 90 per cent of schools. Advice is offered on learning support. Able pupils are reported as being insufficiently challenged.
- ethos – this was seen as consistently good
- accommodation – 25 per cent of schools had problems and 4 per cent had unsatisfactory accommodation overall
- resources for teaching and learning – the supply was seen as good or very good in almost all schools. Staffing standards met or exceeded national standards in all schools.
- management and quality assurance – only 50 per cent of schools had effective procedures to monitor and evaluate their work across the range of curriculum development, teaching and learning, standards of attainment, ethos and management.

STANDARDS IN SECONDARY SCHOOLS

The same HMI report identifies several positive features of secondary schools. These include:

- the quality of teaching and learning – reported as good or very good in 80 per cent of departments

- standards of pupil attainments – S4 pupils sat an average of almost eight Standard Grades each. The proportion gaining Credit awards increased by 4 per cent during 1992–5. In 1995 over 20 per cent of pupils out of 55 per cent gained 3 or more Highers and over 6 per cent gained 5 or more.
- participation rates – 65 per cent of pupils remain in school beyond the statutory leaving age, and 65 per cent of these remain until S6. In 1995 almost 30 per cent of leavers had qualifications which enabled them to enter higher education.
- curriculum provision – all secondary schools had a broad curriculum as nationally defined and all had programmes of personal and social education
- support for pupils – guidance staff provided good support for programmes of positive behaviour in over 85 per cent of schools. There was advice on course choice in almost all schools. Arrangements for learning support staff or others to work with class teachers though cooperative teaching worked well in 75 per cent of schools.
- ethos – the morale of pupils and staff was high and most staff set high expectations of behaviour and performance in class work
- accommodation and facilities – these were reported as very good or good in almost 65 per cent of schools, fair in 35 per cent and unsatisfactory in only a few
- resources – the supply of textbooks, apparatus and items such as audio-visual equipment and micro-computers was very good or good in almost all schools.

This positive picture is balanced by a number of concerns about the attainment and progress of pupils in the first two years of secondary schools. It is reported that pupils are not being sufficiently challenged intellectually. In English language and mathematics pupils in S1/S2 reached the minimum national targets for their stage in only 65 per cent of schools. HMI concerns were given added impetus by the TIMMS study, which found that performance at age thirteen in mathematics and science was significantly below that of many other countries (SOEID 1996a). This disappointing performance was echoed by AAP findings in mathematics which reported performance at S2 in terms of 5–14 levels as weak (SOEID 1996b). The mean score on tasks rated as appropriate for this year group was 47 per cent. The report on science is due in June 1997 (SOEID 1996c). There was sufficient concern about pupils' attainments in mathematics for an HM Inspectorate task force to be set up. The task force has now reported. What action will follow depends on the new Labour government.

A critique of the international comparative studies, AAP and other sources of evidence on standards and quality is outside the scope of this chapter. All approaches to evaluating school, teacher and pupil performance have their strengths and weaknesses. The key points to make are:

- on measures such as participation rates beyond age sixteen and entry to further and higher education, Scotland has much to be proud of
- there is no cause for complacency on attainment in English, mathematics and science, especially in the 12–14 age range
- schools are rising to the challenge of meeting the needs of a wider range of pupils than ever before, but much remains to be done, especially in tailoring the whole curriculum to the needs of pupils of all abilities.

NETWORKING

A stated aim of monitoring pupils' performance is to indicate ways of improving teaching and learning. Monitoring systems, however, *map* performance rather than provide direct practical advice to teachers about teaching methods, curriculum materials or other matters. AAP reports attempt to stimulate teachers' reflection on their teaching by raising issues and questions for teachers to consider. These questions follow reporting of performance in each 5–14 guideline area. In mathematics categories such as information handling, number, money and measurement are used. For example, a recent question on the concept of number was, 'Are S1/S2 pupils, particularly the more able, receiving sufficient teaching of algebra?' On practical aspects of number it was, 'Would pupils' ability to convert between units be improved by more frequent and regular practice in measuring and estimating?' (SOEID 1996b). We do not know how AAP reports are used within schools, but the key point is that attempts have been made to encourage teachers to engage critically with the findings to reflect on their practice. Similarly, Audit Unit reports summarise features of best practice viewed by HMI as a way of prompting schools to consider their own position.

A different approach to encouraging reflection on practice is through alerting schools more directly and immediately to practice elsewhere. The reform of local government in Scotland has been accompanied by a reduction in the number of local-authority advisers and in a redefinition of their role. This means that schools are less able to learn about practice elsewhere in the authority or in the country as a whole. Networking is one response to this, and a number of networks now exist. Details of three are given below.

The Scottish schools ethos network

This network was established to encourage schools to share ideas and experiences about developing a positive ethos. A number of studies of school effectiveness reveal ethos as an important influence on pupils' attainments. SOEID developed ethos indicators and suggested ways in which schools might evaluate their ethos and identify aspects for improvement. The network grew out of schools' use of these indicators, developing them and finding new ways of evaluating their ethos.

The network has over 500 members, including local authorities as well as individual schools. Primaries and their associated secondaries can join as a cluster. For a small fee, members receive a regular newsletter, case studies of school experiences of improving their ethos, regular seminars and an annual conference. There is also a database of members which individual schools can access to make their own direct contacts. The importance of ethos has been signalled by the success of the network in attracting members in just over two years of operation and by the recent announcement of a 'Positive Ethos Award' for the school judged to have made significant efforts to evaluate and improve its ethos.

The Scottish initiative on attendance and absence

This initiative, like the ethos network, aims to encourage schools to share good practice on promoting regular attendance. It publishes regular newsletters, arranges conferences and seminars and provides in-service opportunities for schools wanting to review their policy and practice in this important area. As well as tackling truancy, the initiative raises awareness about issues such as provision for pupils who miss significant amounts of schooling through illness and about school relations with the local community.

The positive discipline initiative

A recently established initiative is that on positive discipline. School discipline is a perennial concern, although research has indicated that it is the drip, drip effect of seemingly small misdemeanours like talking out of turn or work avoidance that is most wearying to teachers. Violence is rare (see Johnstone and Munn 1992). Schools have very little opportunity to share their experience on promoting positive discipline, and this initiative is designed to change that. Working with local authorities, the initiative encourages schools to write brief case studies of their practice, to reflect on key features of their culture which promote good discipline and generally to raise awareness about innovative developments. These include institutionalising praise and rewards through school systems recognising good behaviour, involving pupils and parents in decision-making about school rules and using the expertise of specialist staff to encourage critical reflection on classroom management. Small amounts of funding are available to release staff to write about practice, visit other schools and take part in seminars.

These examples of networking, all given start-up funding by the Audit Unit, are practical ways of encouraging schools to reflect on their practice and to learn from each other. Their starting point is that many Scottish schools are doing excellent work, often in difficult circumstances, and that a powerful way of promoting change is for schools to learn from each other. The networks are at too early a stage to make definitive statements about their success or otherwise, but the ethos network has an evaluation built into its development, practising what it preaches!

CONCLUSION

Standards and quality are emotive topics. This chapter has described pupil attainments in terms of 5–14 levels and in terms of public examination performance at Standard Grade and Higher. Some commentators would question the validity and reliability of conceptualising attainment in terms of levels, and others would question the accuracy of the measures used. The purpose of this chapter has not been to engage in critical debate of these issues, important though they are. Rather it has been to describe current national evidence on attainment, and it has taken levels and measures as unproblematic. This is because we must start somewhere and it would be negligent to ignore a body of information which influences educational policy in Scotland. A third set of commentators would point to the purposes of schooling as being more than promoting academic attainment. Of course, this is true, and one of the important features of HM Inspectorate reports is a concern with guidance, teacher–pupil relationships and ethos as well as with attainment. These areas are not susceptible to measurement in the same way as attainment, but they remain very important features of the educational experiences offered to children and young people.

All countries are concerned with improving the quality of their schooling. If school improvement were easy there would not be the vast literature on it which now exists. There are broadly three approaches in evidence in Scotland, and indeed in a range of other so-called advanced economies. These are:

- to increase competition amongst schools to make them more responsive to consumer demands – a belief in the efficacy of market forces
- to make planning more explicit via the use of performance indicators and targets – a belief in the efficacy of managerialism
- to rekindle the enthusiasm and motivation of teachers for the intrinsic worthwhileness of their work by being explicit about the fundamental goals of why teachers teach and why pupils come to school – a belief in the efficacy of a shared vision of the overall purpose of schooling.

None of these provides a totally satisfactory answer to the question of how to improve schools. Teachers are clearly central. Unless teachers are imbued with a desire to learn, are deeply motivated to do their best for their pupils and feel valued, then schemes for improvement have little chance of success. Scotland is fortunate in having an all-graduate teaching profession, and many teachers undertake advanced training. But much remains to be done. What this might be is to be found in the final chapter.

REFERENCES

Brown, S. and Riddell, S. (eds) (1992) *School Effectiveness Research: Its Messages for School Improvement*, Edinburgh: HMSO.

Croxford, L. and Cowie, M. (1996) *The Effectiveness of Grampian Secondary Schools*, Edinburgh: Centre for Educational Sociology and Grampian Regional Council.

HMI (1991) and (1993) *Using Examination Results in School Self-Evaluation*, Edinburgh: HMSO.

—— (1996) *Standards and Quality in Scottish Schools 1992-95*, Edinburgh: HMSO.

Johnstone, M. and Munn, P. (1992) *Discipline in Scottish Secondary Schools*, Edinburgh: SCRE.

McPherson, A. (1992) *Measuring Added Value in Schools*, National Commission of Education Briefing No. 1, London: National Commission on Education.

SOED (1991) *The Parents' Charter in Scotland*, Edinburgh: HMSO.

SOEID (1996a) *Achievements of Secondary 1 and Secondary 2 Pupils in Mathematics and Science: Third International Mathematics and Science Study*, Edinburgh: HMSO.

—— (1996b) *Mathematics 1994: Assessment of Achievement Programme*, Edinburgh: HMSO.

—— (1996c) *Notice Board: News from the Assessment of Achievement Programme – Autumn*, Edinburgh: SCRE.

Willms, D. (1992) *Monitoring School Performance: A Guide for Educators*, Lewes: Falmer.

9

DEVOLVED MANAGEMENT OF SCHOOLS

Pamela Munn

POLICY BACKGROUND

In the past 15–20 years, policy initiatives in the United Kingdom have been introduced with the intention of redefining the individual's relationship with the welfare state. In many fields of public policy, such as health, housing and education, the relationship has been readjusted by transferring powers from 'producers' to 'consumers' and by changing the nature of accountability. New approaches to management and the introduction of market-orientated policies have been instrumental in this development. In education, devolved management of schools aimed to secure a new form of educational governance by redefining roles and relationships amongst the various interested parties. These include central government, local education authorities, individual schools, teachers, parents and pupils. Devolved management of schools (DMS) is intended to reduce the administrative, financial and political influence of local education authorities by making schools more responsible to parents as 'consumers'. It features four main policy themes:

- increasing competition among schools in attracting pupils, with school budgets largely determined by the number of pupils at the school
- promoting lay, especially parental, participation in school decision-making
- enhancing teachers' and other educational professionals' accountability to parents
- greater delegation of decisions to school level, with local education authorities adopting a strategic and enabling role and providing only a small number of services to schools.

Similar policy initiatives have been adopted in other countries, most notably the United States, Australia, New Zealand and Denmark. Although DMS was introduced as a United Kingdom development, it has been operationalised rather differently in its different constituent parts. This chapter focuses on Scotland, making comparisons with England where these seem appropriate and illuminating. The chapter is in three main sections. First it provides a description of the main policy features of DMS in Scotland. Second, drawing on recent research, it examines how these policies are being perceived by teachers and parents. Finally, it concludes with some speculations about future developments in this area.

KEY ASPECTS OF POLICY ON DMS IN SCOTLAND

There are three main aspects of policy which are worth high-lighting because they are distinctively different from the situation in England. These policy differences derive from and might be seen to reinforce Scotland's collective welfare orientation to the provision of education and the relative autonomy of what McPherson and Raab (1988) define as the 'education policy community'. The collective welfare orientation is a shorthand way of describing traditional values of high-quality education being accessible to all as a democratic right rather than to a privileged few. Although such an orientation has been described as a myth (Gray, McPherson and Raffe 1983), it has a powerful hold on Scots' perception of their education system, and indeed some aspects of the system already described in Chapter 1 support such a perception. Most notable are the small independent sector in Scotland, the disappearance of selection as a means of allocating children to schools and the relatively high participation rates in post-school education, in particular in higher education. Other aspects are less persuasive, such as the setting which takes place in comprehensive schools at fourteen-plus and the in-creasing differentiation of institutions of higher education in terms of quality in teaching and research. Nevertheless, Scotland has adopted a somewhat different approach to DMS from England.

Parental choice

Parental-choice legislation was introduced in Scotland in 1981, but gave stronger rights to choice than the comparable English legislation (the Education Act 1980). The Scottish Act gave parents the right to choose the school attended by their children; education authorities were required to comply unless a statutory exception applied; dissatisfied parents were given the right to appeal to an education-authority appeals committee whose decision in favour of the parent was binding on the authority; and parents were given a further right to appeal to the sheriff against an adverse decision by the authority appeals committee (Adler, Petch and Tweedie 1989). The main differences between Scottish and English legislation on choice are summarised by Adler *et al.* (1989:50–1) as follows: the Scottish legislation emphasised choice more strongly as a right whereas the English legislation stressed that parents had to give a reason for their choice; statutory exceptions were much more specific in Scotland – relating to the need to employ an additional member of staff, or alteration to school buildings or being seriously detrimental to good order and discipline; the Scots had an additional right of appeal to the sheriff; the statutory duties of appeal committees and sheriffs were more strictly defined; and finally, where an appeal is upheld in Scotland, the authority is required to review all similar cases. Parents' rights to choose were strengthened in England in 1988.

School boards and governing bodies

School boards were not established in Scotland until 1988. Before then a secondary school and its associated primaries had a school council whose functions were very limited (see Macbeth *et al.* 1980). School boards' functions are:

- to promote contact between the school, parents and the community and to encourage the formation of a parent–teacher or parents' association
- to approve the headteacher's plans for use of the capitation allowance (typically the budget for books, stationery, equipment, etc.)
- to participate in the selection of senior staff
- to control the use of school premises outside school hours

127

- to set occasional holidays during term time
- to receive advice and reports from the headteacher and, in particular, an annual report which includes a report on the aggregate level of pupil attainment
- to have any matter raised by the board considered by the headteacher and education authority
- to receive information from the education authority about education in the area, including statements about past and intended expenditure on schools.

Their powers over finance are very limited: they have the right to veto the capitation budget (books and materials) set by the headteacher and the right to be consulted about the school budget in general under devolved financial management arrangements. These powers contrast markedly with those of governing bodies, which have statutory responsibilities for hiring and firing school staff, for determining aspects of the curriculum and for school budgets.

The composition of the two kinds of body is different too. Despite the more restricted functions of boards, their role as a prime channel of parental influence is reflected in membership. There are three categories of members, parents, teachers and co-opted. While precise numbers vary depending on school size, parents are the largest single group and command a majority over all other groups combined (Munn 1993). Governing bodies, in contrast, consist of parents, LEA-appointed members, foundation members in the case of voluntary aided schools, teachers and co-opted members (Golby 1993). A potentially significant difference is that headteachers are members of governing bodies whereas they are the 'principal professional advisers' to boards, not members. Local councillors can attend board meetings but cannot vote, and in practice few do so.

Devolved financial management

Although there are many similarities in the general frameworks in which budgetary control is devolved from the local authority to schools, there are also some important differences between Scotland and England at a strategic level. (There are also differences among local authorities.) The main similarity is that the formula by which a school's budget is calculated is pupil numbers. Roughly speaking, the more pupils, the more money a school will attract. The key differences are that in Scotland budgetary control is devolved directly to the headteacher, not to the school board, and that financial formulae are based on actual rather than average staff salaries. This means that there is no imperative to save money by employing inexperienced and therefore cheaper staff as in England, and until very recently most local authorities in Scotland had a no-redundancy policy for teachers. Thus the full force of market imperatives has yet to be felt in Scotland. A school which fails to attract sufficient numbers of pupils to pay for its staff has the safety net of the staff being redeployed to other schools. The time scale is different too. Whereas devolved management of schools was introduced in England as part of the wide-ranging 1988 Education Act, the Scottish equivalent was introduced only in 1993 and will be fully operational in all schools by 1998.

Overview of main Scottish/English differences

To sum up, the main Scottish/English differences in the devolved management of schools are:

- Local financial management was introduced in England by legislation (the 1988 Education Reform Act) reinforced by prescriptive administrative guidelines, whereas DSM was introduced in Scotland by more flexible guidelines without prior legislation.
- Local financial management was introduced in 1990, whereas the first phase of DSM began only in 1993, with full implementation across all schools scheduled for 1998. However, Strathclyde Region, at that time the largest education authority in Europe, had introduced its own scheme in 1990, initially covering six secondary schools and associated primaries.
- Parents constitute a majority of the membership of school boards in Scotland, whereas in England they have no such majority on school governing bodies. Teachers are represented on both governing bodies and school boards, but local-authority nominees can only sit on the former. Headteachers are the principal professional advisers to school boards in Scotland, but are members of governing bodies in England.

129

- Whereas in England, the governing bodies have been given statutory powers on a range of matters including staffing, curriculum and discipline, in Scotland, school boards have a largely consultative role and broadly analogous powers have been devolved to the headteacher.
- Scottish education authorities have more flexibility than their English counterparts in applying their own funding formulae and in devising schemes of delegation to schools. In England, a fixed minimum proportion (80 per cent) of a school's budget is allocated on the basis of pupil numbers weighted for several factors, whereas in Scotland the guidelines require only that the 'bulk of funding' must be allocated on this basis.
- The proportion of education authorities' school budgets delegated to schools must be at least 80 per cent in Scotland, but 90 per cent in England.
- School budgets are delegated to the governing body in England, but to the headteacher in Scotland.
- Scottish schools receive actual salary costs whilst English schools receive average salary costs calculated across the authority as a whole.

In addition to these 'supply-side' differences, there are some important 'demand-side' differences between England and Scotland. All Scottish education authorities initially allocate children to the school serving the area in which they live and then allow parents to make a 'placing request' for another school, whereas many English authorities have abandoned zoning and require all parents to express a preference at the outset. Moreover, the closer links between secondary schools and their associated primaries in Scotland mean that parents are less likely to choose secondaries other than the one associated with their child's primary school. Thus, although parents in both countries have broadly similar statutory rights of school choice, the assumption that children will normally attend their 'local' school is stronger in Scotland. The combined effect of these supply-side and demand-side differences is that competition between schools is more limited in Scotland; Scottish schools are less subject to the discipline of market forces; and parent-members of Scottish school boards are less formally involved in decision-making than are parents on English governing bodies. However, there may well be local deviations from this generalisation.

Three further contextual differences are worth emphasising. First, while a minority of English authorities still provide selective secondary schools and many operate single-sex schools, all state secondaries in Scotland are non-selective and almost all are co-educational. Thus, there are fewer differences among Scottish schools. Second, while more than one in six secondaries in England have chosen to 'opt out' of local authority control and to receive their funding instead directly from central government, only one small secondary and one small primary school in Scotland have done so. Third, in 1996 the two-tier system of local government in Scotland was reorganised, establishing single-tier authorities. This meant that the twelve councils which were formerly responsible for education were replaced by thirty-two. In addition to uncertainties caused by any change in settled relationships, this restructuring will undoubtedly have a consider-able effect on devolved management and other aspects of educational provision. A more piecemeal reorganisation is taking place in parts of England.

PERCEPTIONS OF THE OPERATION OF DSM

One of the major policy aims of DSM was to enhance teachers' accountability to parents. This was to be achieved in a number of ways, two of the most important being the publication of a range of information about schools and the ability of parents to choose schools for their children. The assumptions were that schools which were doing a good job in the eyes of parents would prosper and flourish with increased pupil numbers and larger budgets while schools which were not attractive to parents would have to 'pull their socks up' or close. Information about pupil examination success, progress to higher education and attendance rates was assumed to be important to parents and therefore to influence their choice of school.

Have schools in Scotland been responsive to parental choice? This is a difficult question to answer since in large parts of Scotland geography means that parents have little alternative to the local school. However, parents have been using their right to choose, and the most recent figures on placing requests show that the vast majority of parents obtain their first choice.

Recent research on teacher and headteacher perceptions of DSM (Adler *et al.* 1996) suggests that the importance of pupil numbers in determining school budgets has not resulted in active competition among the small number of schools studied. Schools were aware of the need to enhance their local image, to raise awareness in the local community of what they had to offer. The various ways in which schools did this suggests that they were focusing on presentation rather than substance. The core business of teaching and learning was not directly changed. Furthermore, presentation or marketing effort was not directed at negative campaigning about other schools. Schools which scored well in the national performance tables of examination results did not trumpet their success, but rather tended to underline the partial nature of the information presented in such tables.

Where changes to teaching and learning were perceived, these were in curriculum organisation (such as a move to establish a set of able pupils) or in curriculum provision (such as more technology teaching). The schools studied in the research which responded in these ways tended to be schools in socially mixed catchment areas where there was a view that the school could indeed do something to attract more pupils. The small number of schools in deprived areas in the study tended to believe that there was little or nothing they could do to prevent the decline of their roll. There was also an impact on the hidden curriculum, with schools becoming alert to the importance of school uniform as signalling a particular ethos which they believed would be attractive to parents. Similarly, there was a recognition of the importance of discipline and attendance for the school's image. While it would be foolish to attribute these concerns only to parental choice, it cannot be discounted entirely as an influence. Indeed, several commentators have pointed to the increasing numbers of pupils being excluded from school as evidence of the impact of parental choice on schools. Exclusion can be a way of signalling to parents that a school is maintaining high standards of discipline.

A second policy aim is to increase lay and especially parental participation in school affairs. One of the most important structural ways of promoting such participation has been through the establishment of school boards. As mentioned above, the guidelines introducing DSM delegated financial decision-making power to the headteacher, not to the school board, but the guidelines also suggested that headteachers would consult with boards about their spending plans. Has DSM resulted in greater involvement of boards in decision-making than hitherto?

The only major research to date tackling this question is that undertaken by Adler *et al.* (1996). They conclude that DSM has not had a substantial impact on the work of school boards, or on boards' relations with headteachers. This research is illustrative, consisting of a study of six boards in secondary schools in different parts of Scotland, and so the findings are not generalisable. They are, however, congruent with those of other research on the work of school boards (see, for example, Munn 1993; McBeath 1993). A common finding of such research is that boards and governing bodies exhibit strong trust in the headteachers' professional expertise and judgement. In the case of DSM, headteachers typically presented reports on various aspects of school life, including general budget statements, spending on materials and equipment, staffing changes and so on. These were discussed to varying degrees, but the headteachers were never seriously challenged about the way in which they wanted the schools to develop. In Adler *et al.* 1996, there was no evidence that board members were either actively involved in initiating policy at school level or more generally involved in policy formulation by presenting significant challenges to the headteachers' proposals. Very few schools had parent representation on school development planning groups, for instance, and those that did so had headteachers who were committed to an open and consultative management style rather than for any other reason.

The general reluctance of boards to become involved in school decision-making is summed up in the following extract from an interview with a parent member:

Parent: From a school board point of view, it [approving capitation or spending priorities] really becomes a kind of . . . talking shop. . . . We can sit for hours talking about £50 here and £100 there, but really at the end of the day . . . they are the professionals – they know what is best, to a great extent. I wouldn't go down to the doctor's and start telling them, 'You should be spending £100 on this rather than that.'

Interviewer: Well, it could be said they are experts at teaching and this isn't teaching. . . . I mean whether money should be spent on redecorating the entrance hall or on computers . . . it is not just a teacher's

Parent:

decision. Parents will have a view too, and their view may be equally important.

That's in an ideal world. . . . How did school boards come about in the first place? Is it to do with parental choice or is it to do with political ideology? My own view is that school boards could be abolished tomorrow and I don't think the education of our children would be compromised particularly.

School boards have been more active as pressure groups on local and national government policies. Examples include school refurbishment programmes, the need for a new school fire alarm, and the general level of resourcing of education. Furthermore, national and local government now recognise school boards as a force to be reckoned with when large-scale policy change is planned. Parents are represented on the Scottish Consultative Council on the Curriculum, for instance, and on the Higher Still strategy group (see Chapter 5). Some local authorities hold regular meetings with school-board representatives to explain policy, implicitly recognising the need for school-board support or acquiescence if policies are to be carried through. Many authorities now have in post 'Parents' Officers' whose role in part is effective communication with parents via school boards and other channels. I have argued elsewhere (Munn forthcoming) that lay participation in the education policy process at school-board level is essentially one of being informed about developments. Evidence suggests that the use which school boards make of this information is largely dependent upon the advice of the headteacher. Thus boards tend to react to policy initiatives taken elsewhere and to be guided by the headteacher's interpretation of the salience of the policy initiative for the school and hence for what parents might do.

FUTURE DEVELOPMENTS

The general intention of DSM to transform the culture and working relationships of schools through mechanisms such as parental choice, the establishment of school boards and devolving financial decision-making from education authorities to schools has had partial success in Scotland. Parents have certainly exercised their right to choose, school boards have been established in the overwhelming majority of schools, and head-teachers have now taken responsibility for managing their school budgets. Yet the balance sheet is modest against the broad and ambitious policy goals which DSM embraced.

Evidence from school boards shows that providing opportunities for a more collective role for parents at the school level is no guarantee that they will either be taken up or used. The deference shown to headteachers and the trust in their expertise cast doubt on the currently fashionable notion of active citizenship. Stewart (1996) argues that participation at local level is within the compass of citizens and that 'they can exercise control over decisions on the smaller scale of matters important in their daily lives' (p. 39). Yet voice options are difficult to exercise in the context of schools, which are inherently undemocratic institutions. Furthermore, the current emphasis on school accountability through performance indicators of various kinds, expressed numerically, encourages a reliance on experts to interpret their meaning. This, combined with the general trust in the professional competence of head-teachers, operates against real decision-making by school boards. It is difficult to see this situation changing.

Schools have become more demonstrably aware of the importance of parents to school budgets by a school-funding formula based on pupil numbers. Schools have, accordingly, taken pains to present themselves more attractively to parents, to raise awareness of what they have to offer. Some, indeed, have made important changes to curriculum organisation and provision in a bid to attract more parents to their schools. Ball (1990) points to a situation in England where schools are choosing parents rather than vice versa as popular schools become oversubscribed and cannot expand provision to meet demand. This is not the situation to any great extent in Scotland, and it has been interesting to observe the reluctance of headteachers whose schools appear at the top of national performance tables actively to trumpet their success. Their typical reaction has been to cast doubt on the validity of the measures used.

The myth or reality of the tradition in Scotland of access to high-quality education as a right for all can work in two ways. First, it can be used to justify pupil selection so that the child from the humblest home gets the opportunity to study in the best schools (and has access to the great universities). These arguments can be seen in justification for the assisted places scheme, for instance, whereby able children get financial help to enable them to attend independent schools. Second, it can be used as an argument for improving all school provision and for ensuring that all schools provide opportunities for children to progress to further and higher education. This sense of schools all being engaged in the same enterprise perhaps explains to some extent the marked reluctance there has been in Scotland for schools actively to compete against each other in the quest for pupils.

Thus, the prediction is for little to change dramatically in schools' relationships with parents or indeed in relationships among schools. What is more likely is a continuing diminution in the role of education authorities as providers of direct services to schools, begun under DSM and continuing with the restructuring of local government. The unknown influence is the impact of the establishment of a Scottish Parliament. A Parliament may reinvigorate democratic participation in the institutions of civil society, and this may in turn have an effect on school boards, making them more involved in decision-making. Social science, unlike the natural sciences, cannot predict effects with certainty. We must wait and see.

ACKNOWLEDGEMENTS

This chapter draws heavily on the work of two projects researching DSM and on working and published papers arising from these projects. The first project was funded by the Economic and Social Research Council (R000233653) in 1993–6 and the team consisted of Michael Adler, Margaret Arnott and Charles Raab at the University of Edinburgh and Lucy Bailey and myself at Moray House. The second project was funded by the Scottish Office in 1995–6 and involved Lorraine McAvoy at the University of Edinburgh as an additional member of the above team.

REFERENCES

Adler, M., Arnott, M., Bailey, L., McAvoy, L., Munn, P. and Raab, C. D. (1996) *Devolved Management in Secondary Schools in Scotland*, Final Report to the Scottish Office.
—— with Petch, A. and Tweedie, J. (1989) *Parental Choice and Educational Policy*, Edinburgh: Edinburgh University Press.

Ball, S. (1990) 'Education, inequality and school reform: values in crisis!', Inaugural Lecture, Centre for Educational Studies, King's College, University of London.

Golby, M. (1993) 'Parents as school governors', in P. Munn (ed.) *Parents and Schools: Customers, Managers or Partners?*, London: Routledge.

Gray, J., McPherson, A. and Raffe, D. (1983) *Reconstructions of Secondary Education: Theory, Myth and Practice since the War*, London: Routledge & Kegan Paul.

McBeath, J. and Thomson, W. (1993) *Making School Boards Work*, Interchange 16, Edinburgh: Scottish Office.

Macbeth, A. M., McKenzie, M. L. and Breckenridge, I. (1980) *Scottish Schools Councils: Policy Making, Participation or Irrelevance?*, Edinburgh: HMSO.

McPherson, A. and Raab, C.D. (1988) *Governing Education*, Edinburgh: Edinburgh University Press.

Munn, P. (1993) 'Parents as school board members', in P. Munn (ed.) *Parents and Schools: Customers, Managers or Partners?*, London: Routledge.

—— (forthcoming) 'Parental influence on school policy: some evidence from research', submitted for publication.

Stewart, J. (1996) 'Democracy and local government', in P. Hirst and S. Khilani (eds) *Reinventing Democracy*, Oxford: Blackwell.

137

10

POLICY-MAKING IN SCOTTISH EDUCATION

A case of pragmatic nationalism

Lindsay Paterson

INTRODUCTION

Scottish educational policy-making is relatively independent of that in the rest of the United Kingdom. This chapter traces the development of that autonomy since the middle of the twentieth century, looks at the tensions between Scottish and United Kingdom policy-making that have grown since 1979, and speculates about possible directions in which Scottish educational policy-making might move over the next few decades. The main attention here is to the school sector.

The chapter is not just a description, however: it is also an attempt to explain. Explanation of a system of government probably seems more urgent in small nations like Scotland than in large states (although that may be changing as Europe converges, a point to which I return at the end). Although the daily practices of Scottish education – as in other countries – can proceed in ways that take the Scottish framework for granted, issues of policy in Scotland always raise questions about why the system is distinctive at all, and whether it will continue to be separate. The organising idea around which a tentative explanation is built in this chapter is that of negotiated autonomy.

To illustrate in a preliminary way what I mean by that, we can start by giving one apparently obvious answer to the question of why Scottish educational policy-making is somewhat independent at the end of the twentieth century. It is independent (we might suppose) because it always has been. This can be called the explanation by origin. The most frequently heard version of it is that Scottish education is independent because its autonomy was built into the Union between the Scottish and English Parliaments in 1707. Education was one of the areas (along with the church and the law) which the Scottish negotiators insisted on reserving to Scotland. But other versions can also be found. For example, in 1996, we often heard reference being made to James IV's Act of 1496, by which the state required the sons of freeholders to be schooled so as to be equipped to rule the country. This Act, it is often suggested, created a precedent for a public system which the Reformation of 1560 then reinforced and which the Union and various further Acts from 1872 to 1980 confirmed. So, according to this kind of answer to the question 'why independent?', Scotland has a separate system for governing education at the end of the twentieth century because it has always had one: autonomy today is explained by the simple fact of autonomy yesterday.

There are two comments to be made about that kind of explanation. One is that it is very popular, and probably always has been since the Union itself. Every time there has been debate about Scotland's place in the Union, we can find people citing the special status of Scottish education in the Union settlement as a reason why Scotland ought to have some formal political control of its own destiny.

But the other point is that such an explanation is inadequate: origins and reproduction are not the same. Pointing out where a set of social institutions originated is important, but it does not explain why they have survived, or how they have been modified to take account of successive waves of social change. So we need also some elaboration of the ways in which the autonomy that was secured for Scottish education in 1707 has been renewed or diluted time and time again. When we try to do that, we face a deeper dilemma, because the type of further explanation that is plausible at any particular time will itself have been shaped by the particular popular explanations that are currently in vogue. So, although – as we will see below – some parts of an explanation lie in theories of pluralism and of corporatism, these now seem pusillanimous compared to the popular appeal of the theory based on the founding status of the Union itself. In an earlier age (and still to some extent today), another explanation might have suggested that Scotland needed a separate system of educational governance because the system of education itself was distinctive – for example because it was smaller, or more democratic in spirit, or whatever. But that explanation too does not really work any more, because it begs the question of how these allegedly distinctive characteristics emerged.

The broad explanation that is offered here cannot help but start from the very popularity of the explanation by origin, and cite nationalism as the organising principle around which an explanation of recurrently renegotiated autonomy can be constructed. Thus an appeal to a founding moment for Scottish educational policy-making – whether that be 1707 or earlier – has indeed frequently proved to be highly efficacious politically, securing a continuing autonomy for the system in a process of obscure bargaining with the United Kingdom.

So negotiated autonomy in the sense I intend here involves two important elements. The first is rational pragmatism. At least since the eighteenth century, and the Enlightenment with which the Scottish elites identified enthusiastically, the Scots have always placed 'reason' above national sentiment as such. In the era of the welfare state, one interpretation of reason has been maximising the resources that are available to fulfil specific goals in public welfare. This interpretation has come about because the political and social forces which created the welfare state were dominated by an ideology of technocracy: social problems were believed to be amenable to rational solution, often explicitly by the application of science to human affairs (Marwick 1964). In that sense, Scots have not differed fundamentally from other social groups: pluralistic bargaining over how to allocate resources in a way that meets agreed goals has become a characteristic feature of the policy process in all the liberal democracies (McLennan 1989). Thus Scotland has become something like a large interest group within the United Kingdom state. It is because of the sanction of 'reason' that Scots have, on the whole, been satisfied with this position (Paterson 1994), and have not opted for the grander historical projects which classical nationalism seemed to offer small nations (Nairn 1995): if a partial autonomy can get certain mundane things done (such as run a functioning education system), then demanding more independence seems rashly romantic.

But – as we will see more fully below – one of the problems with a purely formal pluralist theory is that it does not pay enough attention to where power lies. That brings in the second element of negotiated autonomy, a version of nationalism. This has been the social force that has set the whole process going and has maintained it in existence. The reason why it is possible to talk of a

'Scottish interest' is nationalist pressure, and nationalist sentiment of some sort thoroughly permeates the networks of Scottish government. It permeates, moreover, implicitly – as a background or an ethos of which the actors are mostly not conscious except at moments of overt conflict with England. This Scottishness is therefore an excellent example of what Billig (1995) calls 'banal nationalism' – not usually flag-waving, but flags hanging silently to remind people that they are Scottish. In holding this taken-for-granted national allegiance – and in being able to draw on the broad popular sense of national identity – Scottish governing groups have shared in a common feature of the modern state. In particular, the welfare state was everywhere a national project, and – in the era of mass democracy to which it was responding – achieved legitimacy partly through constructing a popular sense of the national interest (McCrone 1992). In Scotland, however, the national interest which was mobilised was not only British, and indeed has become less and less British since the 1970s. Scottish politicians of all parties have been able to call on an alternative national allegiance to force the United Kingdom state to concede resources and power. In that sense, the banal nationalism of Scottish education also reveals a gap in Billig's analysis: Scotland shows that implicit national allegiance can relate to a cultural grouping that does not constitute a state in the conventional sense, but is, rather, a semi-independent part of another state (Paterson 1994).

SCOTTISH EDUCATION AND THE UNITED KINGDOM WELFARE STATE

Someone looking at the political structures of the United Kingdom in the middle of the twentieth century might be puzzled by a claim that there was a distinctive system of governing in Scotland. There was no separate legislature there, and – until the late 1960s – the party system in Scotland seemed to be broadly the same as in England (Brown *et al.* 1996). That puzzlement might be based on the tenets of liberal democracy, according to which the processes that matter in developing policy are found in Parliaments and in the competition among parties that seek election to them. But that account of policy has long since been found severely lacking. When we move beyond it, the idea that the United Kingdom was a unitary state with one policy process becomes untenable.

Consider three other perspectives on the policy process, and what they have to say about the nature of Scottish government as it evolved with the welfare state. The first is pluralism (McLennan 1989; Jordan and Richardson 1987). According to that, policy is made by the bargaining which goes on among interest groups, only one of which is Parliament. In Scottish education, almost all these groups other than Parliament itself were Scottish rather than British, and indeed until the 1960s Parliament paid almost no attention (McPherson and Raab 1988). At the centre of the process was the Scottish Education Department (SED); it was part of the Scottish Office and was overseen by the Secretary of State for Scotland, a member of the United Kingdom Cabinet. The SED had two main arms, the administrative civil service and the inspectorate. Between them they set up a dense network of committees, and they maintained official and informal contacts with pressure groups, with representatives of local government, and with professional associations. McPherson and Raab (1988: 472) have described these as the 'policy community', the Scottish instance of British pluralism.

The SED could not impose its will on that policy community: notably, it had to negotiate with local government (which actually ran the schools) and with the representatives of teachers, primarily in their main trade union, the Educational Institute of Scotland. For example, a historian of the Association of Directors of Education in Scotland (the chief education officers in the local authorities) could write in 1989 that:

> the unique and central place occupied by the Association in the fashioning of the education structure . . . could well support a view that an account of the Association's activities . . . would directly suffice as a history of the state provision of public education in Scotland.
>
> (Flett 1989: ii)

In return for granting this key role to leading professional bodies, the SED obtained access to the educational expertise which these groups embodied, and also gained their consent to changes. Thus much of the detailed work involved in developing the system was undertaken by *ad hoc* working groups or committees of enquiry, or by the Advisory Council on Scottish Education (until the early 1960s), or by a plethora of permanent public bodies – for example the Scottish Examination Board (providing mainly academic examinations), the Scottish Vocational Education Council (mainly vocational assessment), and the Scottish Consultative Council on the Curriculum. All these bodies included a mixture of SED personnel and people from other organisations.

The purposes of the networks were expressed in the usual terms of political rationality: to improve the quality of education, to equip young people for changing labour markets, or to contribute to the economic efficiency of Scotland and the United Kingdom. Thus we can find aims and methods in official reports that could be reproduced almost anywhere. For example, the 1965 Memorandum of the SED which officially promoted child-centred methods in primary schools was expressed in the internationally recognisable language of progressive education (Darling 1994).

But permeating these networks – and grounding the rationality – was an assumption of a fairly homogeneous Scottishness, and a view of Scottish education as having certain distinguishing features, notably that it was democratic, intellectually rigorous and of high quality. McPherson and Raab question whether these were 'myths' or accurate representations of reality, but they do not doubt the powerful emotional hold they had on the policy-makers. For example, in the debate about comprehensive education in the 1960s, each side tried to claim that its model of secondary schooling was the true inheritor of the Scottish 'tradition' of educational democracy. The proponents of selection argued this on the grounds that rigorous meritocracy allowed the efficient detection of talent in all social classes; people who favoured the abolition of selection wanted to reinterpret that Scottish tradition in a more egalitarian way. Thus, insofar as the governing system was pluralist, it could not help being imbued with Scottish national sentiment because it was firmly embedded in Scottish civil society.

Furthermore, insofar as pluralism is not a wholly satisfactory way of characterising the process, the nationalism becomes all the more inescapable. The main critique of pluralism is that it neglects the different amounts of power which the groups have: allegedly it is too formal as a theory, describing a network of groups without paying attention to which social interests they represent. One response has been the theory of corporatism, which accepts the pluralist critique of liberal-democratic theory, but insists that government remains the most powerful group in the bargaining process (Jordan and Richardson 1987). Alternative theories of corporatism differ as to the relative power of the state: 'liberal' versions claim that interest groups voluntarily maintain a close relationship with the state, while 'authoritarian' accounts suggest that the state can impose its will. But all the theories share the view that the state guides the process. Indeed, most of the other groups depend for some of their legitimacy on the government's recognition of their importance. In Scotland, the members of the national committees and so on mostly do not get there as of right, but have to be invited by the SED. The groups then become the agents through which the government's will is implemented.

McPherson and Raab (1988) conclude that the Scottish system became increasingly corporatist in the 1960s, as the power of the SED increased. The partnership they describe

> resembles corporatism in the exclusiveness of its relation-
> ships, in its assumption that mutual interests outweigh the
> partners' separate or conflicting interests, and in the sharing
> of authority.

(p. 473)

This 'mutual interest' is another way of putting the sense of a Scottish national interest. The SED, represented politically by the Secretary of State, could become the national leader, especially in bargaining with the Treasury. For example, McPherson and Raab quote Bruce Millan (Secretary of Sate, 1976–9) as telling them that the Scottish Office was left to sort out by itself the consequences of changing patterns of expenditure. The scope for this autonomy increased from 1978 onwards when, in anticipation of the setting up of an elected Scottish Assembly, the Secretary of State was given power of vires over most of the Scottish Office's block grant from the Treasury. Lying behind Millan's comment is an unquestioned national framework, in which the Secretary of State speaks for Scotland and has the authority to decide what is in Scotland's best interests. If that convention were not acceptable within Scotland itself, then it would not work as a negotiating position around the Cabinet table (Levitt 1992).

In thus leading the definition of the Scottish interest in education, the SED could find a ready ideological support in nationalism, which remained a centralising force within Scotland at least until the 1960s. Not only did the key social elites which dominated the corporatist bargaining share a homogeneous view of the national identity; they could persuade others to accept it as a means of presenting a united front to London. Although this national unity was mainly about negotiating within the United Kingdom state, it resembles the centralising tendency of nationalism in all nations, the imposition (partly by negotiation) of a single national culture on the nation as a whole (Gellner 1964). It was thus a kind of 'official nationalism' (the term coined by Kellas (1991)), even though Scotland did not have a separate state of its own. In the era of corporatist bargaining, the multi-national United Kingdom state was able to promote distinct national projects in its component parts.

Furthermore, whatever the process by which national decisions are made – pluralism or corporatism or something else – there remains the large area of implementation, the means by which the national policies have an impact on children's learning. As Hogwood and Gunn (1984) argue, 'perfect implementation is unattainable', because all policy proposals have to be modified in practice when placed in the hands of professionals such as teachers, and when faced with the complexity of society and of individuals. The arm of the SED which has most to do with implementation has been the Inspectorate, and in that sense the SED has been able to keep some control of the process. But the inspectors have always themselves been educational professionals, and so their negotiation of practice with teachers has been shaped by a shared professional outlook. They have also had to deal with the local directors of education, also from the same professional background. Schools themselves, in any case, had a great deal of scope to devise their own ways of responding to national policies, although – because of the centralising effects of the Inspectorate and the Scottish Examination Board – they tended to follow a common pattern to a greater extent than did schools in England and Wales.

Again – as with pluralism and corporatism – this is a source both of rational pragmatism and of nationalism. Most of the daily policy discussion in which Scottish teachers and others engage has been similar to the discussion that could be observed in other similar educational systems. In the 1940s, for example, this would have been about the themes of education for all; in the 1960s it would have been about comprehensive education; and at any time it would also have been about details of the curriculum, assessment and educational psychology. But, at the same time, the educational professionals have taken for granted a Scottish frame-work – articulated through their trade unions, their professional associations or their statutory accrediting body, the General Teaching Council – and they have shared with the policy communities the inherited myths about the distinctive character of the system, and therefore have voluntarily participated in disseminating a homogeneous image of Scottish national identity. In this respect, Scottish teachers have been no different from other segments of Scottish society in the welfare state, sharing the sense of a Scottish national interest that government should serve, and affirming that national framework implicitly, through a 'banal nationalism' of the type documented by Billig (1995). All these groups have participated in the common project of periodically using nationalist assertion as a way of putting pressure on the United Kingdom state – via the Scottish Office – for what they feel to be adequate treatment of Scottish interests.

TENSIONS IN THE GOVERNMENT OF SCOTTISH EDUCATION

Many of the structures described in the last section are still in place. Even under a Conservative government that has been described as hostile to Scottish distinctiveness, pluralistic relation-ships survived, and implementation had to be taken into account even by the most zealous of reforming ministers. Much of this continues to happen in a fairly low-key way. For example, the entire reform of post-16 certification in the mid 1990s (Higher Still) is being undertaken with almost no direct political interference, as a matter of consultation among the SED, the examining bodies, the Curriculum Council, the local authorities, and so on. But the system has experienced unprecedented strains since the late 1970s, some resulting directly from the confrontation between a right-wing government and a left-of-centre Scottish civil society, and some stemming from more general tendencies in the welfare state. As in the earlier period, however, these new processes can be best explained in terms of negotiated autonomy: there is both a continuation of the rational pragmatism and an intensification of the pervasive nationalism, but the nationalism has itself started to take a more plural and contested form.

This is seen most straightforwardly in the confrontations with the Conservative government since 1979. Although the govern-ment was never popular in Scotland (Brown *et al.* 1996), it managed to avoid serious conflict in education until the late 1980s. The crucial change came about when the third Thatcher government turned its attention firmly to social policy. This was a project that was directed at Britain as a whole, and in some respects has been more thorough in England and Wales than in Scotland. For example, the introduction of market forces into education has gone further in the South, through, for example, what amounts to the privatisation of the Inspectorate, the system of local management of schools and the incipient encouragement of schools to alter their entry criteria in order to allow competition in the kinds of education they offer. None of these has happened to the same extent in Scotland, and yet the analogous legislation has provoked deep hostility because it is believed to threaten the integrity and autonomy of Scottish education. The government was seen as trying to take over the policy communities, either by placing its own supporters in positions of influence or by ignoring the old channels of consultation. It was also accused of undermining the autonomy of local government, by controlling its expenditure, by surrounding it in regulations, and – eventually, in 1996 – by abolishing the 9 large and powerful Regions which had administered education since 1975, replacing them by a fragmented system of 29 new authorities.

Two examples illustrate the impact of the Conservative government on policy-making in Scottish education, and the reactions to it. The first concerns vocational education, one of the earliest efforts by the Thatcher government to reform the school system: it resulted most directly after 1984 in the Technical and Vocational Education Initiative (TVEI), a scheme devised for the whole of Britain, and presided over by the Sheffield-based Manpower Services Commission. In Scotland, such a body was widely greeted with horror, on three main grounds (Fairley and Paterson 1991). The first was that it was unnecessary: it was held that Scotland already had a better balance between academic and vocational education than England, so that reform could proceed incrementally. The second was that it threatened comprehensive education by raising the possibility of an invidious vocational track. And the third was that it by-passed the usual channels of Scottish government in the Scottish Office. As a result of these reactions in the policy community, the SED was able to block the introduction of TVEI for one year. In the time it gained, the Inspectorate constructed a broad consensus for its own scheme of vocational education, which resulted in the Scottish Vocational Education Council and its system of national certificates. When TVEI was admitted, it therefore had to accept this system, and also was required to accept the emerging Standard Grade examinations which had begun to replace the old Ordinary Grade. Alongside this manoeuvre by the SED, the schools and local authorities were also able to shape TVEI to their own ends because it was decentralised. Thus any threat which it might have posed to comprehensive education could be averted, for example by insisting that all pupils be exposed to its programmes.

The story of TVEI illustrates well the workings of Scottish negotiated autonomy. On the one hand, the debate was mostly about pragmatism, not overtly about nationalism – about looking at what kinds of course would be suitable for the growing proportion of young people who were staying in education beyond age sixteen. The responses, on the other hand, were not specifically Scottish, in the sense that the new vocational courses mostly contained nothing that marked them out as different from similar courses in other countries. But, as always, the Scottishness can be found in the context. Three strands of nationalism were mobilised. There was a reference to an old 'tradition' – that Scotland dealt quite well with vocational education. There was reference to a new one, too – that comprehensive education was now definitely popular in Scotland and embodied characteristically democratic approaches to education. And there was the centralising willingness to fall into line behind the SED in order to avoid being imposed upon by a body based in England.

Of course, since this was a negotiation and not a rebellion, a central principle was conceded, namely that there needed to be a greater vocational emphasis. But the outcome was not only a sense that the policy community had successfully resisted external interference. More lastingly important was the new system of courses and assessment which is now contributing to the more general reform of post-sixteen education. As on many previous occasions, and not only in education, the outcome of one episode in the negotiation of Scottish autonomy has been a strengthening of the separateness of Scottish government.

The second example of resistance to the Conservative government is that of school boards. Scottish schools have not traditionally had governing bodies of the type that are long established in England and Wales, and so the inauguration of boards in 1989 was castigated as an alien import, especially since a majority of the members of each board were to be elected representatives of parents of current pupils. Combined with the policy of parental choice of school (which had been implemented in a radical form in Scotland in 1981), the parent-dominated boards were believed to put public education at risk. The reasons for suspicion were increased by the policy's apparent provenance in New Right thinking: the Scottish Education Minister at the time was Michael Forsyth, an enthusiastic Thatcherite. And yet the story of school boards since then has been quite different from what the New Right might have wanted, or what the initial critics feared. The boards have been captured by Scottish civil society as a way of extending popular participation in educational policy-making. Parent members have, generally, been supportive of professionals, and have used the boards to defend public provision in the face of further radical proposals from the government (Munn forthcoming). The most notable instance of this occurred when the boards, together with groups representing parents, led the opposition to primary-school national testing in the early 1990s, forcing a government retreat.

Once more, this experience combined pragmatism with nationalism. It was pragmatic in that the main arguments which defeated primary-school national testing were about its lack of educational merit: these arguments were not directly about anything distinctive in Scottish education. But it has also been about nationalism, because the whole policy of national testing was believed to be an attempt to anglicise the system. The policy community was mobilised in defence – notably the Association of Directors of Education, the Educational Institute of Scotland and representatives of parents. They were acting to defend a valued Scottish tradition of child-centred primary education, even though that dated only from 1965: nationalist myths do not have to be ancient to have the political power of ancient beliefs. The system has been left with an addition to the policy process – the school boards – which have been captured as a way of expressing the system's desire for political autonomy.

So conflict with the Conservative government produced opportunities for the old workings of Scottish educational policy-making to be renewed. The main change in this respect has been the more frequent instances of confrontation over fundamental matters. Although overt conflict between a government and the education system had happened before, and had led to government defeat, these earlier episodes had not seemed to threaten some of the system's core values. For example, the Labour government was forced to retreat from its attempt to close some colleges of education in 1977 in the face of widespread campaigning (Marker 1994). But however important the colleges may be, they can hardly be said to be central to popular perceptions of Scottish education. The direct impact which the primary testing issue had on many thousands of parents, in every Scottish community, is of a quite different order of significance.

This growing confrontation has left a legacy of mistrust, and so has contributed to the slow decay in the legitimacy of the United Kingdom state in Scotland. One of the reasons for the current intense debate about a Scottish Parliament is the feeling that the United Kingdom is no longer able to promote or even tolerate diversity in its component parts (Crick 1993). The educational conflicts have not only been specific instances of this; because of the centrality of education in Scottish identity, they have been prime sources of it as well.

However, the Conservative government has not been the only source of decay in the current system of governing Scottish education. Equally important have been tendencies that can be found throughout the liberal democracies, tendencies towards democratisation and accountability in public services. This has involved not only a critique of the hierarchy and secrecy of the state, but also a rejection of corporatism, and of pluralism too. Even in a policy-making process in which the state does not control everything, the people who actually take part in political bargaining are not socially representative: they tend to be from social elites, no matter how sincerely they claim to speak for the disadvantaged (see, for example, Giddens 1994). As Hirst has put it:

> modern publics have become more demanding, better educated, and less deferential. Their attitude to public services has changed from one of gratitude to a consumer consciousness. They demand higher quality and also more diverse services of greater complexity.
>
> (1995: 344)

These attitudes, and the political responses to them, have been found as much in Scotland as elsewhere (Fairley and Paterson

1995). As elsewhere, too, they are opening up the governance of the welfare state to unprecedented public scrutiny, not only at a national level, but also at the levels of local authorities and individual educational institutions. Despite the widespread suspicion of the Conservative government in Scottish education, some of the changes it brought about have in fact helped this new democratisation to be expressed – for example through school boards, which do allow for wider participation than was possible before, even though they (like all elected forums, in education or elsewhere) remain dominated by the well educated and the relatively affluent (Munn 1993). The Conservative government also contributed to developing a more plural version of Scottish identity, through, for example, investing large amounts of money in Gaelic-medium education.

There are two particular effects of democratising pressures in Scotland. One reinforced the opposition to the Conservative government, in the sense that the part of Scottish government that seemed to be most in need of accountability was the Scottish Office itself. Although the SED might still frequently have been able to present itself as speaking on behalf of Scottish education, it remained under the control of a ministerial team which had not been able to command a majority of the popular vote in any test of public opinion since 1979. The argument that a Scottish Parliament is needed to democratise the Scottish Office long pre-dates the Conservative government (Paterson 1994). It is in fact the Scottish instance of the post-1960s scepticism about bureaucracy which can be found amongst thinkers and politicians of both the left and the right (Giddens 1994).

The other effect of pressures towards democracy brings into question the whole system of Scottish semi-autonomy, challenging the various social elites that have constituted the policy community. As Humes (1986) and others have noted, 'the leadership class' in Scottish education has been deeply conservative in many respects, and has been as socially unrepresentative as its counterparts elsewhere – male-dominated, middle-class, white, defensive, and by no means encouraging of popular participation. Humes also notes (1995) that even a radical right-winger such as Michael Forsyth (Secretary of State, 1995–7) was not able seriously to challenge this entrenched elite. As a result, much of the debate about a Scottish Parliament has concerned how to establish new types of democracy (Brown et al. 1996). The image of the national identity which accompanies such debates is more fractured and decentralised than the old one. The old official nationalism remains, but it has to some extent adapted to new social conditions, so that, for example, even a Scottish Office dominated by the Conservatives could attempt to select members of the leadership class from a wider range of backgrounds (Scottish Office 1993, para 9.8). But that system of patronage is itself challenged by a variety of social movements asserting the rights of particular groups. Thus the women's movement in Scotland claims a right to be different from its English or American counterparts, but, at the same time, and above all, asserts that its vision of Scottish identity is radically different from the old official one, and even from more long-established oppositional cultures such as that of Scottish Labourism (Howson 1993). In particular, in the making of policy for education, the argument has been put that including more women would lead to a greater diversity of styles and outcomes (Macintosh 1993).

UNDERSTANDING THE FUTURE

The forms which educational policy-making are likely to take over the next few decades thus depend on wider constitutional and social developments. If a Scottish Parliament is established, then the policy process is bound to become more transparent, especially if the pressures for radical democratisation have any influence. Even under an unreformed constitution, change cannot be avoided, because the broader tendencies towards democratising and decentralising the welfare state are bound to continue in the United Kingdom as elsewhere. But, whatever the changes, the framework that has been proposed for analysis in this chapter will continue to help to explain Scottish policy-making, for three main reasons.

The first is that all political communities are now having to engage in negotiation, because social, economic and political life is increasingly characterised by interdependent relationships. There is an unresolved debate as to whether the process is best described as 'globalisation' (the development of a single world economy) or as 'internationalisation' (the intensifying involvement of still autonomous national economies in a world system). But that matters less here than that the changes involve increasingly dense networks of cooperation, influence and control among nations and states (Hirst and Thompson 1996). This is most obvious in the European Union, where even the countries that used to think of themselves as sovereign are having to adapt to a world of bargaining. In that context, the skills which Scottish education has established in negotiating with the United Kingdom will be valuable; in particular, they would allow a Scottish Parliament to maintain a greater degree of autonomy than those who distrust European integration might fear – just as the autonomous Parliament of Catalonia has done.

The second is that rational pragmatism will not come to an end. However many doubts may have been expressed about the Enlightenment model for conducting human affairs, it still commands support that is much too broad – and has been much too effective – to disappear quickly (Paterson forthcoming). In particular, therefore, the daily practices of policy-making in education will still mainly be about setting goals and evaluating these in terms of their direct impact on teaching, learning and attainment. Because of the universality of such criteria and methods, a large part of Scottish policy-making will continue to look very like that in other places.

But the third reason is that nationalism, far from falling into disuse, is proving much more able to adapt itself to a new social order than its main rivals as challenges to unfettered capitalism, socialism and communism. It is certainly true that nationalism of the old sort is decaying. The over-arching project of establishing a nation-state is rarely now plausible, even though it remains attractive to some (as can be seen in Bosnia and Northern Ireland). But the nationalism in which a place like Scotland has always engaged has become more important, as a means of relating people's identities to broad political processes, but not as an engulfing identity which excludes all others (Brown et al. 1996). If people are more inclined to want a say in the government of the public services, then they also want a choice in how the national identity is formed, and then this new identity becomes a collective basis for the new systems of government.

If that analysis is correct, then one final conclusion is that Scottish experience has a lot to offer other places. Learning to negotiate and learning ways of relating political processes to individual identities are problems which Scottish education has had to cope with for some time, and are common problems now faced by policy-making throughout the new Europe.

ACKNOWLEDGEMENT

This chapter has benefited from the advice of David McCrone and Pamela Munn.

REFERENCES

Billig, M. (1995) *Banal Nationalism*, London: Sage.
Brown, A., McCrone, D. and Paterson, L. (1996) *Politics and Society in Scotland*, London: Macmillan.
Crick, B. (1993) 'Essay on Britishness', *Scottish Affairs* 2: 71–83.
Darling, J. (1994) *Child-Centred Education and its Critics*, London: Paul Chapman.
Fairley, J. and Paterson, L. (1991) 'The reform of vocational education and training in Scotland', *Scottish Educational Review* 23: 68–77.
—— (1995) 'Scottish education and the new managerialism', *Scottish Educational Review* 27: 13–36.
Flett, I. (1989) *Association of Directors of Education in Scotland: The years of Growth, 1945–1975*, n.p.: Association of Directors of Education in Scotland.
Gellner, E. (1964) 'Nationalism', in *Thought and Change*, London: Weidenfeld and Nicolson, pp. 158–169.
Giddens, A. (1994) *Beyond Left and Right*, Cambridge: Polity.
Hirst, P. (1995) 'Quangos and democratic government', *Parliamentary Affairs* 48: 341–59.
Hirst, P. and Thompson, G. (1996) *Globalisation in Question*, Cambridge: Polity.
Hogwood, B. W. and Gunn, L. A. (1984) *Policy Analysis for the Real World*, Oxford: Oxford University Press.
Howson, A. (1993) 'No Gods and precious few women: gender and cultural identity in Scotland', *Scottish Affairs* 2, Winter: 37–49.
Humes, W. (1986) *The Leadership Class in Scottish Education*, Edinburgh: John Donald.
—— (1995) 'The significance of Michael Forsyth in Scottish education', *Scottish Affairs* 11: 112–30.
Jordan, A. G. and Richardson, J. J. (1987) *British Politics and the Policy Process*, London: Unwin Hyman.
Kellas, J. (1991) *The Politics of Nationalism and Ethnicity*, London: Macmillan.
Levitt, I. (1992) *The Scottish Office, 1919–1959*, Edinburgh: Scottish History Society.
McCrone, D. (1992) *Understanding Scotland*, London: Routledge.
Macintosh, M. (1993) 'The gender imbalance in Scottish education', *Scottish Affairs* 5: 118–24.
McLennan, G. (1989) *Marxism, Pluralism and Beyond*, Cambridge: Polity.
McPherson, A. and Raab, G. (1988) *Governing Education*, Edinburgh: Edinburgh University Press.

Marker, W. (1994) *The Spiders' Web? Policy Making in Teacher Education in Scotland, 1959–1981*, Glasgow: Sales and Publication Department, University of Strathclyde.

Marwick, A. (1964) 'Middle opinion in the Thirties: planning, progress and political "agreement"', *English Historical Review* 79: 285–98.

Munn, P. (1993) 'Parents as school board members: school managers as friends?' in P. Munn (ed.) *Parents and Schools: Customers, managers or partners*, London: Routledge.

Munn, P. (forthcoming) 'Parental influence on school policy: some evidence from research', submitted for publication.

Nairn, T. (1995) 'Upper and lower cases', *London Review of Books*, 24 August: 14–18.

Paterson, L. (1994) *The Autonomy of Modern Scotland*, Edinburgh: Edinburgh University Press.

—— (forthcoming) 'Individual autonomy and comprehensive education', *British Educational Research Journal*.

Scottish Office (1993), *Scotland in the Union: A Partnership for Good*, Edinburgh: HMSO.

11

HOW SCOTTISH IS THE SCOTTISH CURRICULUM?

And does it matter?

Cameron Harrison

> (I)t is to the advantage of England that the Welsh should continue
> to be Welsh, the Scots Scots and the Irish Irish. . . . There may be
> some advantage to other peoples in the English continuing to be
> English. . . . If the other cultures of the British Isles were wholly
> superseded by English culture, English culture would disappear too.
> (T. S. Eliot, 'Notes towards the definition of culture')

NATIONAL IDENTITY AND THE CURRICULUM

This chapter reflects on the nature, content and structure of the
Scottish school curriculum in order to illustrate aspects of the
important relationship between national identity and national
school curriculum. It is not a systematic description of the overall
pattern of the Scottish school curriculum: the reader must seek
such a description elsewhere (for example Harrison 1994). Rather,
this chapter is an exploration of aspects of the relationship
between national culture and national identity: in a Scottish
context, certainly, but, I hope, pointing to issues of relevance to
educators in all nations.

One important point must be made at the outset. It relates to
the notion, central to this chapter, of national identity. I cannot
emphasise too strongly that, when I use this expression, I do not
refer to any narrow notion of group identity, let alone superiority,
asserted in political or ethnic terms. The identity of a people lies in
its culture, not in its gene pool. And therein lies the significance of
the issue at the heart of this chapter: since, if the matter of
national identity is to be understood in cultural terms, then the
role of the nation's education system in shaping and forming that

culture becomes a matter of considerable importance. It becomes a matter of vital concern to understand the ways in which aspects of the national milieu are reflected in, and consequently shaped by, the education of the nation's young people.

The education of the young is the fulfilment of the covenant between generations. It is in the provision of education that we offer to our young people the best that we ourselves have garnered from our fathers. We introduce to them the knowledge and ideas which have illuminated and enriched our lives: we seek to develop in them the skills and capabilities which we have learned are of use, and which have given us our present quality of life; we offer them the best of our values and beliefs, and hope that they will surpass us in the task of living in the light of them; and we do all of this in a process which we hope will deepen their understanding and enlarge their humanity. We call this process education, and we set up schools and employ teachers to put it into effect.

Education, then, is concerned with the transmission of culture and of capability; with the development of the individual, and with a sense of belonging; and the school curriculum is the vehicle for this process. The school curriculum is the answer to the questions, 'What should go on in schools?' and 'What should children learn?' And so the nature and the content of the curriculum matters. It reflects the values and priorities of the nation and it helps to shape the nation's future. To say this is not to ignore the failure of attempts at using schooling as short-term social engineering – that is a different issue: it is to acknowledge the power of ideas and ideals on the minds and lives of the young. Nor is an assertion of the importance of the school curriculum a pretence that there are no other significant influences at work shaping the lives and futures of our young people. It is simply to point to its relative importance in the complex dynamic of forces at work in this arena – and not always at work for the best. For we cannot claim that the influence of schools and of the curriculum on our young people is always an unqualified good.

> If there are in this country too many people who fear what is new, believe the difficult to be impossible, draw back from responsibility, and afford established authority and tradition an exaggerated respect, we can reasonably look for an explanation in the institutions that moulded them.
>
> (Smout 1987: 229)

157

CAMERON HARRISON

CULTURE AND CAPABILITY

One of the principal roles of an education system, then, is to transmit culture and capability through the generations. The bulk of this chapter considers the relationship between more conventional views of culture and curriculum. Let me, first, give some attention to the notion of capability as an aspect of culture, and to the relationship between each and the curriculum.

The material wealth of a nation, and the quality of life of its people, are heavily dependent on the capacity of its people to create wealth. But such a capability is not simply a matter of possessing a technically skilled workforce; there is also the question of human disposition. The stunning explosion of industry in Scotland in the nineteenth century was a product of many factors. Some were certainly geographical, some geological; some were economic, some political: but one of the most critical factors was the existence, to an extent equalled in few other nations in the world at that time, of a broad sector of well-educated, capable men ready and eager to play their part in this revolution. And it is important not to underestimate the importance of that word, *eager*; because their willingness to act was just as important as was their capacity to do so. The national culture and the national education system had combined in Scotland to produce a substantial tranche of men who valued both presbyteries and profits (Marshall 1992). Because of their education and their theology – and the two were closely linked – these men possessed both the abilities and the disposition to create wealth. And they did. Living and working in a society which did not simply value the acquisition of knowledge and skills, hard work and commitment, but which, through church and school, made the creation of wealth not simply possible but a moral imperative, these men, supported, and sometimes driven, by their womenfolk, 'redeemed the time, because the days were evil!' And in the exceptionally unlikely economic soil of this poor part of a peripheral island, they made the desert to bloom.

There is a general lesson here. Porter (1990) asks a telling question:

Why do some social groups, economic institutions, and nations advance and prosper in international economic competition – and others fail?

And he answers:

158

the most important aspects are attitudes towards authority, norms of interpersonal interaction, attitudes of workers towards management and vice versa, social norms of individualistic or group behaviour and professional standards.... These in turn grow out of the education system, social and religious history, family structures, and many other intangible but unique national conditions.

The relevance of the point, and therefore the importance of the issue, is, I think, self-evident.

HOW SCOTTISH IS THE SCOTTISH CURRICULUM . . .

Back, then, to the issues central to this chapter. I want to address this question in three ways. First, I examine the Scottishness of the *content* of the curriculum; second, I look at its *nature*, the educational ideas and concepts used, often implicitly, but always powerfully, to frame, design and describe the curriculum for teachers and for schools; and third, and briefly, I describe the nature of the national *change and development processes* themselves – the characteristic manner in which the curriculum is developed.

. . . IN ITS CONTENT?

One of the principal purposes of education is to help young people make sense of their society, to understand why it is the way it is, and to reconstruct from where have come those values and norms which underpin the expectations and patterns of behaviour which are part of their everyday life. If young people are to be able to understand who they are, if they are to make sense of the context and communities in which they live, they must have an opportunity to understand the cultural soil from which they have sprung.

Language and literature

The starting point for any such discussion must surely be a consideration of the place of both Gaelic and Scots language and literature in our schools. It is important to begin on a positive note. That is because, while few would deny that much has been done in recent years to help support and enlarge the place of both these areas of the school curriculum, many would argue that such current attention no more than begins to make up for the neglect, indeed active persecution, which these areas suffered in the past. That may be so; nevertheless, it is important to note that the age of hostility is past. The current debate recognises the importance of these matters; at issue now is only the nature and extent of the support to be given – determining the best way forward.

But, even given the positive steps taken in recent years, there are those who remain sceptical about the desirability of such actions. Their queries, too, are important and deserve respect. 'Why preserve a faltering language?', they ask. Or even, 'Why attempt to revive a dying one?' These questions demand sound answers – especially in a time of economic stringency and curriculum overload.

And such questioners have a point: without doubt, problems do exist. For example, current writing in Scots, and to a slightly lesser extent in Gaelic, is of mainly one sort: it is expressive, rather than transactional or discursive. In both tongues our poetry is flourishing and our creative writing and story-telling are acquiring a new life. There are, however, no parallel developments in the broader fields of writings about ideas. No one is writing about economics in Scots: there are no Ph.D. theses in physics being crafted in Gaelic. The volumes in the excellent New History of Scotland series (1992) are written (much to the surprise of my Dutch friends) not in Scots, but in English, and (to their utter astonishment) no one in Scotland even seems to regard that fact as worthy of notice, let alone regret. Why is this so? The reason is not, as some have asserted, that either of our native tongues is in some way deficient or inadequate in the language of discourse. No, the reason is much simpler, much more powerful and, sadly, much more inexorable. The lifeblood of intellectual growth and the development of ideas is the process of discourse. The exchange of ideas, debate, challenge, agreement, dissension, consensus all require an appropriate vehicle for communication and access to a wide audience. In medieval Christendom the vehicle was Latin; in our time it is English.

Scotland, of course, has both benefited and suffered from its close linguistic ties with England. We have benefited in that we are able to piggy-back on the international currency of our near neighbour's language and its rich literature – and being so closely related to Scots, at least it is eminently accessible to us. Would

Walter Scott have had the phenomenal effect on European culture and literature which he has if he had been writing in Gaelic? I fear not.

But there is a corresponding disadvantage to our close linguistic relationship. If our language had been more significantly different from English, perhaps the seventeenth century would have seen a Scots Bible, as it saw a Welsh one. That one step would have made such a difference. As it was, the inexorable pressure mounted – remember that Davie Hume died confessing not his sins but his Scotticisms – and now we are faced with the formidable task of restoring not only to currency, but to respectability, a tongue which has for generations been presented in public as the language of the comedic, the nostalgic or the hopelessly maudlin. Frankly, our Gaelic cousins have in many respects an easier task.

The case for despondency is not overwhelming, however. That is because, in an interesting irony, the forces of history may be on the side of threatened, minority languages. All over the world – excepting, of course, in the United Kingdom and former colonies – the power and pervasiveness of the English language are working a change. The youth of nation after nation is, both by national educational policy and by the ease of international communication, becoming bilingual. Nor, by and large, is this seen in most developed countries as a threat (set aside France for the moment), but as a political, cultural and economic necessity – for the youth, indeed, it is often *fait accompli*. Across Europe, *governments* and educators see *both* the importance and the advantages of the adoption of English *and* the vital importance of preserving their own tongues. Last year, the Netherlands Parliament was within a whisker of passing a law insisting that in future all, as opposed to most at present, instruction in science in their upper-secondary schools should be in English. But at the same time they insist on providing for linguistic diversity even within their own small country – the Friesians of north Zeeland are consistently and powerfully supported by their national government in their own language not only as a legitimate subject of study, but also as a medium of instruction. A recent encounter with thirteen leading figures from the national education system in Albania revealed that all of them had read *Ivanhoe*, in English, at school. Rob Roy too, even before the film, was a 'weel kent cheil in Albanian schools; though whit they made of Andra Fairservice I'd like fine tae ken!'.

All over the developed and developing world the same trend is evident: linguistic confidence is reflected in an eagerness to carry forward national tongues and, at the same time, gain access to the advantages of the new international lingua franca – English.

But perhaps the history of language in Scotland holds lessons for all nations world-wide. Perhaps the international drift towards English in academic discourse, in science and technology and in business and commerce really does present long-term challenges to non-English-speaking nations. Perhaps, even more, the growing dominance of English in the field of entertainment and in the increasing permeation of the Internet both as a means of communication and as a medium of distribution presents not just challenges but threats to local linguistically framed lines of cultural and literary heritage. The lesson from Scotland is certainly that this can be the case – but that it need not be so. Although we were dangerously late to act, our experience is that national language and literature *can* flourish *alongside* English; and that in doing so, they can enrich and illuminate the lives of a country's young people. But to ensure that this happens, we have found, does require active curriculum planning on the part of schools – and real support nationally in the form of advice and resources. The key to tackling this problem is a confident realisation that defence against the powerful and pervasive effect of international English is neither possible nor, probably, desirable; but that active and appropriate intervention can ensure parallel language development; and that in this way the curriculum, and thus the culture, of the nation will be enriched and not impoverished.

History and society

How can young people growing up in Scotland understand their society, or indeed their environment, without knowing of the forces, from within and from without, which have shaped our poor and privileged nation: our brotherhood and our enmity with our southern neighbours; our periods of war and our times of peace; our rough wooings and our eventual contract of marriage? How can our young people understand the society of which they are part unless they have opportunity to understand the forces which have formed it? They live in a society shaped by theology and by industry, by prophets and by profits. Why do these grand gothic Victorian churches stand at every street corner of wealthy west-end city suburbs – and why two church buildings, if seldom now two congregations, in hundreds of tiny villages up and down our country? What did the Scottish Enlightenment do to world thought and what did it do to the poor Scots tongue? Why do Glasgow, Edinburgh and Dundee all have two major football teams (*pace* the Jags!) and Aberdeen only one? What circumstances led to Scotland's transformation from a kind of medieval Albania to having one of the highest, if not the highest, per capita incomes in the world by the last quarter of the nineteenth century? What processes, at home and abroad, have taken Scotland, tiny Scotland, from being the place where, at the turn of the century, half the world's shipping and a third of its locomotives were being manufactured to where we are today – a country with no steel industry, though a promising silicone one? How did it happen that, in the early part of this century, and all over the world, the words 'quality' and 'reliability' conjured up to the world an image not of Japanese motor cars but of Scottish ships? What on earth has happened since?

The opportunity to develop such understanding demands a central place for history, and for Scottish history within the curriculum. But not just any Scottish history. A history which is comprehensive, in that it reflects all the major events and processes which shaped our nation and our society. A history which is both a vehicle for the education and development of the individual and, as importantly, offers the information and ideas which will allow those young people to make sense of who they are and of their society. Not a 'here's tae us' history, celebrating the undoubted, indeed astonishingly disproportionate, contribution of this small nation of ours to modern thought and achievement; but a history which seeks to understand equally our successes and our failures, our triumphs and our guilt. Not an exclusive, scotocentric view of history, but a history which, having established a sense of process and chronology, having told the whole broad tale, constantly sets local and national events and processes in the context of, and connects them to, events and processes in the rest of Europe and the rest of the world.

... IN ITS NATURE?

It is not just in its content that our school curriculum is Scottish. It is also characteristically Scottish in its design. One of the striking facts which emerge when the Scottish school curriculum is compared with that in any other part of the United Kingdom is that it appears to be constructed with reference to different design principles. For example, in Scotland, where a child-centred educational philosophy was adopted more cautiously, though perhaps ultimately more thoroughly, than in England, the primary-school curriculum is organised in broad 'curricular areas'; in England it is organised in subjects. That difference respects a conviction in Scotland, slowly acquired but now firmly held, that it is important for the curriculum, and the process of learning, to respect the child's experience and view of the world (see Chapter 3).

I want to point to two other significant differences in the way in which the Scottish curriculum is constructed. I have chosen these areas not just because they are important in their own right but because they reflect significant aspects of our culture and of our evolving beliefs about education.

Breadth and balance

The first is the issue of breadth and balance in the curriculum. Now, breadth and balance are matters which have become almost a shibboleth in Scottish education. Scots generally assert that our school curriculum discourages narrow specialisation – especially in comparison with most other parts of the United Kingdom. We claim adherence to the broad liberal ideal, and insist on breadth of experience and on coverage in the curriculum of all important areas. In some respects, of course, we live up to this ideal. Thanks mainly to the Munn committee (SED 1977) of the mid 1970s, to the efforts of the Scottish CCC since, and, crucially, to the support of HM Inspectorate, Scottish curriculum guidelines for primary and for secondary education to age sixteen currently ensure that a significant measure of breadth and balance in the curriculum is experienced by all our young people. However, not everything in the garden of the curriculum is rosy. The Howie Report (SOED 1992) on the future of upper-secondary education in Scotland came in for a good deal of sharp criticism in certain crucial aspects. Its ill-thought-through proposal to divide young people into two streams, academic and vocational, met, quite correctly in my view, with overwhelming rejection. But in one other regard Howie launched a devastating critique of our present system – one which has not received the attention it deserved. The issue is that of breadth and balance within the area of the fifth- and sixth-year school curriculum. The committee had two main lines of criticism. First it pointed out that there was a great deal more narrow specialisation amongst students taking Highers than we were pretending. English, mathematics, physics, chemistry and biology was a not uncommon grouping – particularly amongst certain sectors of students. On the other hand variations on the English, history, geography, French and German theme were far from infrequent. Worse than that: comparing our upper-school curriculum with that of our continental neighbours, Howie launched a devastating attack on our very concept of breadth. We had no answer.

So how Scottish is the Scottish curriculum in this regard? Compared with the English ours is very Scottish – if that isn't Irish. But compared with our own aspirations – not to say our liberal traditions and former good practice – we are weighed in the balance and found wanting.

Academic and vocational

Which brings me to my second point. I return to Howie's concern to 'bridge the academic–vocational divide': to 'create parity of esteem between academic and vocational courses'. This is an exceptionally interesting issue: it illustrates sharply the importance of keeping a canny ee on the ideas we use as the coinage of our thought – particularly as we try to frame a problem. Let me borrow an example from higher education in order to illustrate what I mean.

Two years ago, my son – like so many other young reprobates before him – completed an honours degree in law at Edinburgh University. Now, was that an academic or a vocational course? The answer is, of course, 'Yes! – that course is highly academic *and* highly vocational.' Whence came this idea that vocational and academic qualities are dichotomous? The university Scot of the nineteenth century would have stared in incomprehension at anyone who voiced such ideas. Learning in Scottish universities then was highly academic – in the sense that the knowledge was pursued rigorously, objectively and, if necessary, for its own sake. And this was done in the context of institutions and courses which were very highly vocationally focused (Walker 1994). The two aspects of life and of learning were seen as being of equal value and, as important, as being both coexistent and interlinked.

> The same age, which produces great philosophers, and politicians, renowned generals and poets, usually abounds with skillful weavers and ship carpenters. We cannot reasonably expect, that a piece of woolen cloth will be brought to perfection in a nation, which is ignorant of astronomy, or where ethics are neglected.
>
> (David Hume in Scott (1993))

From where has this misleading idea come, then – this notion of the academic being an exclusive alternative to the vocational? The answer to this question, regrettably, does not reflect well on the Scots. The hollow, but disabling, vocational/academic controversy is a straightforward reflection of a very class-specific value system which was not native to Scottish culture, but which has been enthusiastically imported by sections of our aspiring social elite. The vocational/academic schism reflects another nation's system in which, in relatively modern times, the two great universities served primarily as finishing schools for the gentry. At the same time in Scotland, the ancient universities, while probably sustaining higher academic standards, were unashamedly vocational. They were the pathway into the professions: law, medicine and the church – and for the 'sticket', there was always teaching. In England the oldest universities, and the exclusive, expensive, private schools, served as both the guardians of privilege and as gateways for the aspiring upwardly mobile – at least those who could afford the price of entry. They were a port of entry to respectability, to a stratum of society where the very worst sin was to earn your own living. The archetypal product of this system was the effortlessly accomplished amateur, with no visible means of support and a contempt for anything useful – in art or in life. We see the powerful, and damaging, inheritance of that value system still today in what Hutton (1995) calls the *rentier* society – the gentlemanly capitalists – the present-day elite of our system. And this false academic/vocational dichotomy has, I regret to say, become a British, and not simply an English, trait. The impact is evident in our own society and our own education system.

How Scottish is the Scottish curriculum? It pains me to say so, but we Scots have fallen from grace – and in a most uncharacteristic manner. We have failed to examine and question the ideas we have been using to shape our thoughts and our actions. It will not be easy to recover this lost ground.

. . . IN THE PROCESSES ADOPTED TO PRODUCE AND DEFINE IT?

There is a third sense in which the question 'How Scottish is the Scottish curriculum?' can be asked: it focuses upon the method by which national guidelines for the school curriculum are produced. This may at first glance seem to be a peripheral issue; in fact it is central to the main point.

A range of factors have shaped Scottish practice in developing national guidelines. Key amongst them is the keen interest, and confidence, in their education system felt by the overwhelming majority of Scots. One important consequence of this is the significant measure of community of interest felt between teachers, parents and others. Another is a strong expectation on the part of a range of stakeholders – parents, churches, business and commerce and other community groups, as well as teachers – that they all will, as a matter of right, participate in the process of debate about policy development and change. Important, too, has been the powerful role played by teachers, and teachers' associations, in the processes of educational development. Through their local authorities and schools, they expect to be involved – indeed, they recognise their role as the main engine-room of the improvement process. Finally, the role played by central bodies and individuals in positions of national leadership is significant. Such key players would claim to take care to go with the grain of public and professional expectations, rather than against it. There is probably a strong element of truth in this assertion, though perhaps not as much as is claimed. Above all, these various participants, while frequently in conflict, have never become ideologically disengaged from each other, and the protagonists in the debate have always felt it their obligation to take account of the critiques mounted by their opponents, whether professional or political.

Thus, the national processes for curriculum change and development in Scotland might be characteristically described as widespread and vigorous debate, accompanied by an earnest search for partnership and consensus. The size of the country – 5 million people, 405 secondary and 2,500 primary schools – has undoubtedly enabled this process; nevertheless, it is difficult to avoid recognising, in its nature, a reflection of other aspects of national culture. It would be quite misleading to claim that in these arrangements Scotland has a democratic process for development, in the parliamentary sense – actually, it may be better and more effective than that. If, however, Scotland has been able to retain and develop quality within its schools and its education system, it is in part at least due to the fact that our *modus vivendi* has enabled us to avoid some of the sillier educational over-indulgences, and consequent hysterical over-reactions, seen elsewhere.

Of course, a commitment to the principle of consultation and involvement as a human value is only part of the reason for this state of affairs. There is also on the part of those in positions of leadership a clear – and very pragmatic, and Scottish – recognition that the nature of the processes of education are such that, if *real* improvement is to be sought, then all participants must understand and agree how it is to be brought about. In this case we do not have to make a virtue out of a necessity: the two already coincide. Thus, for reasons of both principle and praxis, the processes of improvement within the education system in Scotland can be said to have a distinctively Scottish flavour. If the outcome is not satisfactory to us, then it might fairly be said to be mostly our own fault.

NATIONAL IDENTITY UNDER THREAT?

I suppose that no contemporary discussion of national identity and a national curriculum could be complete without at least a reference to the processes of increasing internationalisation – the feared global homogenisation of culture, and thus identity. This process is seen by many, particularly in some other parts of the United Kingdom, as a threat. It will be evident from this chapter that I do not share that view. My own belief is that, no matter what happens to the political system within the United Kingdom or within Europe, an inexorable consequence of developments in the media and in communications will be to encourage in people a sense of identity simultaneously more local and more international. Already as a consequence of this process, Western Europe, at least, is, arguably, composed of peoples increasingly conscious of their own identity in a way which is at the same time respectful of that of others – we are learning to value our differences. I see the patterns of school provision and curricula reflecting these patterns of distinctiveness in a positive and inclusive way. And that is perfectly congruent with the nature and purpose of education. For it is the task of schools not only to preserve the past, but to enrich the future.

REFERENCES

Harrison, C. E. (1994) in *Briefings for the National Commission on Education*, London: Paul Hamlyn Foundation.

Hutton, W. (1995) *The State We're In*, London: Vintage.

Marshall, G. (1992) *Presbyteries and Profits*, Edinburgh: Edinburgh University Press.

New History of Scotland series (1992), Edinburgh: Edinburgh University.

Porter, M. (1990) *The Competitive Advantage of Nations*, London: Macmillan.

Scott, P. (1993) *A Concise Cultural History of Scotland*, Edinburgh: Mainstream.

SED (1977) *The Structure of the Curriculum in the Third and Fourth Years of the Scottish Secondary School* (the Munn Report), Edinburgh: HMSO.

Smout, T. C. (1987) *A Century of the Scottish People*, London: Fontana.

SOED (1992) *Upper Secondary Education in Scotland: Report of the Committee to Review Curriculum and Examinations in the Fifth and Sixth Years of Secondary Education in Scotland* (the Howie Report), Edinburgh: HMSO.

Walker, A. L. (1994) *The Revival of the Democratic Intellect*, Edinburgh: Polygon.

12

FUTURE DIRECTIONS?

Pamela Munn

Crystal-ball gazing is for astrologers. It is a dangerous activity for social scientists. This chapter is necessarily speculative, drawing on three overlapping themes of the book. These are respectively curriculum provision, school organisation and policy-making in education.

CURRICULUM PROVISION

The curriculum in many stages of education is going through substantial change, and we can expect this to have a significant impact well into the next century. Perhaps the most important change is in upper-secondary education, with the attempt in Higher Still to devise a unified curriculum and assessment system to cover all academic and vocational education beyond S4. As Raffe (in Chapter 5) highlights, the key to this strategy is the single ladder of progression and attainment, in marked distinction from most other countries' approaches. The establishment of vocational and academic tracks has been firmly rejected, as has the establishment of separate schools for academic and vocational courses. Higher Still will have a far-reaching effect on upper-secondary provision by offering a flexible and diverse curriculum in terms of courses and levels to the increasingly diverse range of students choosing to stay on at school beyond age sixteen. It is noteworthy, for instance, that it is the first reform to include the concerns of young people with special educational needs, right from the start.

A key element in Higher Still's success will be the attitude of higher-education institutions (HEIs) to the qualifications gained. If they focus on qualification levels of aspiring students, rather than on the number of attempts and length of time taken to achieve the qualifications, the reform has the power to transform education radically. It has, for example, the power to puncture traditional notions of ability, in a way that no amount of academic writing on the topic can. The idea that ability is innate and fixed and can be measured by means of cognitive attainment tests at specific ages would increasingly be held in question if HEIs took a liberal view of Higher Still qualifications. Will they? I myself am cautiously optimistic. HEIs are admitting a larger number of students than ever before with non-traditional qualifications and many operate accreditation of prior learning schemes for older students with few or no traditional entry qualifications. HEIs are thus gradually becoming accustomed to a more diverse student population than hitherto not only in terms of age but also in terms of entry-level qualifications. Furthermore, if Scottish Group Awards or Intermediate 2 level qualifications (see Chapter 5) gain entry to HNC and HND courses, alternative routes into universities are sustained by links between these courses and degree-level courses in the second and third years. We may see an expansion of existing links which largely concentrate on engineering degrees.

Thus higher education through its admission criteria has, as always, the power to influence dramatically what is taught and regarded as important in the school curriculum. Higher Still can be seen as pivotal reform, opening up access to higher education to a more diverse range of the population than ever before. On the other hand, it may increase the stratification of HEIs with the traditional Scottish universities remaining more conservative in their admissions criteria than the newer institutions. In that case, 'real' or 'quality' higher education would remain in the cultural possession of an elite, as Halsey (1991) has argued.

Higher Still also has a potential backwash effect on Standard Grade. Is it possible that Intermediate 1 and 2 levels might be taken by 14–16-year-olds? Boyd (Chapter 4) reminds us that the Howie committee, set up to review upper-secondary education, suggested that in time Standard Grades might be taken at the end of the pupils' third year rather than the fourth. It is clear that Standard Grade will come under increasing pressure for review, being squeezed between the 5–14 Programme on the one hand and Higher Still on the other. This prediction is given greater force by current concerns about under-achievement in general, and in science and mathematics in particular, in S1 and S2. This implies that the curriculum provision and organisation for 12–14-year-olds will be a focus for attention with questions being raised about the overcrowding of the curriculum (fifteen plus subjects) and about the efficiency of mixed ability teaching (HMI 1996). Thus Standard Grade might well be under pressure from each end of the secondary-school curriculum, an increasingly squeezed element of the 12–18 curriculum provision.

It is likely that we will see continuing expansion of pre-fives education, and a continuing concern with standards of literacy which will, no doubt, encourage the expansion of early intervention projects designed to improve reading and writing by targeting children in disadvantaged areas in nursery and in the early years of primary. Evaluations of these projects in Edinburgh and elsewhere suggest promising short-term results in terms of the raising of reading ages, although their long-term effects are more doubtful. (See Fraser 1997 for a review.) We may witness a move towards more family literacy programmes in the future. These programmes 'identify the family as a whole as the site for educational intervention' (Tett 1997) unlike more recent approaches which focus on either children or adults. An emphasis on families would be consistent with attempts to encourage greater parental involvement in their children's schooling and with concerns to raise the basic skills of adults – a multi-dividending approach.

Family literacy programmes, of course, raise fundamental questions about whose literacies count, and as Barton (1995 quoted in Tett 1997) points out, 'Dominant literacies originate from dominant institutions of society. Vernacular literacies have their roots in everyday life.' This is clearly not the place to engage in debate about literacy, but it does lead to questions about the distinctively Scottish nature of the school curriculum. This is so because the dominant language of instruction in Scottish schools is English and will remain so. As the Scottish Consultative Council on the Curriculum (SCCC 1996) has pointed out, Scots vernacular is the language of the home for many people, and yet the curriculum sends important messages that this mode of speech is inferior to Standard English. The SCCC has tried to provide resources for teachers wishing to introduce children and young people to Scottish literacy and cultural traditions. It has also revived the place of Scottish history in the curriculum and is currently engaged in widespread consultations on the extent to which Scottish culture, in the broadest sense, pervades and should pervade the curriculum. This concern with Scottishness and the curriculum will probably continue. The creation of a Scottish Parliament would give it added impetus, but so too would the failure to create one, given the balance of political opinion in Scotland. (See Chapters 10 and 11.)

A future direction which has remained relatively unexplored in this book is the place of new technology in the curriculum. The development of ever more sophisticated computer hardware and software and multi-media resources seems to have out-stripped our abilities to use these resources effectively across the curriculum. A particular concern is the initial and continuing professional education of teachers so that they are alert to the potential uses of IT and can experiment with ways of integrating these kinds of resources into their classroom practice. This is by no means only a Scottish concern (European Union 1997). Thus alongside changes in the organisation of teacher education in terms of new partnerships between schools and teacher education institutions, referred to in Chapter 7, we are likely to see changes in the teacher education curriculum. In addition to a concern with new technology, there is likely to be a move towards more subject-specialist education for primary teachers, particularly in mathematics and science, and more management training for intending headteachers, given their increased responsibilities under devolved schoolmanagement.

SCHOOL ORGANISATION

There are no 'grammar' schools in Scotland within the maintained sector, despite the fact that some schools have 'grammar' or 'academy' in their title. It is easy to forget how relatively recent a phenomenon the widespread establishment of comprehensive schools is. McPherson and Raab (1988) remind us that it was not until 1974 that the vast majority of Scottish secondary pupils (85 per cent) were in six-year comprehensive schools. Scotland started on comprehensive reorganisation in 1965 with more schools that were omnibus (taking children regardless of their ability, although streaming them) and pursued a narrower range of organisational options for comprehensive schools than south of the border. Nevertheless, by 1970 there were still 138 four-year schools offering O Grades (McPherson and Raab 1988: 134). Furthermore, legislation was necessary in 1968 to enforce the abolition of fees in selective secondaries in Glasgow and Edinburgh.

Thus the abolition of selection and the disappearance of different kinds of secondary schools for children of different ability do not have a long history in Scotland. Place this alongside the existence of grammar schools and selective entry for sizeable proportions of pupil entry in England, Wales and Northern Ireland, and one is left wondering how robust comprehensive education in Scotland is.

Theories of intelligence as innate and fixed advanced in the 1920s and 1930s have proved remarkably resilient despite the work of, for example, Gardner (1993) and Goleman (1996) and recent brain research (Healy 1990; Jensen 1994). One can see that under present curriculum and assessment arrangements it would be perfectly possible to stratify the school population in terms of 5–14 levels A–E and to use, say, a composite of English, mathematics and environmental studies grades as the basis for selective entry. Our current preoccupation with individual competition adds weight to such a scenario. Theories of intelligence, after all, individualise success or failure and divert attention from between-group inequalities in provision. We see the same phenomenon at work in demonising badly behaved children – 'the pupils from hell'. Thus the possibility of a return to more differentiated forms of schooling should not be dismissed lightly.

On the other side of the balance sheet, however, comprehensive education in Scotland can claim some notable successes. Key amongst these are the increasing proportion of children gaining qualifications at age sixteen and the proportions continuing with education beyond the statutory leaving age. It is also noteworthy that Paterson (1997) detects an increase in the numbers of young people from working-class backgrounds entering higher education and a narrowing of differentials between the socio-economic status of entrants to higher education. The percentage of working-class entrants to higher education, for example, rose from 8 per cent in 1980 to 15 per cent in 1994. (For more detail see Paterson 1997: 32–3.) This increase can be explained partly in terms of the rising aspirations of this social group, in itself perhaps a consequence of the increased educational opportunity of parents, and partly by the expansion of supply in higher-education places. Furthermore, a return to a selective system would inevitably raise questions about resource differentials, teacher status and the self-esteem of the young people in the different kinds of schools.

If a return to selective schools does not take place, will we see increasing curriculum differentiation among children attending omnibus schools? HMI is sending mixed messages to the teaching profession about the efficiency and effectiveness of mixed ability teaching. On the one hand, it advocates setting in *Achievement for All* (HMI 1996), and on the other, it advocates multi-level teaching in *Higher Still* (Scottish Office 1994).

According to Gamoran (1996) 'a rich and rigorous academic curriculum promotes high levels of student achievement and curriculum differentiation is associated with achievement inequality'. Analysing the effect of Standard Grade on student achievement and attainment in 1984–90 he concludes that inequality within schools declined because 'disadvantaged students had better opportunities to enrol in academic courses and they usually obtained awards in the subjects they studied' (p. 15). Before the introduction of Standard Grade, less able students had few opportunities to demonstrate achievement since its predecessor, the O Grade, was designed for a small percentage of students. Gamoran did not detect any effect of Standard Grade reform beyond secondary school in terms of increasing equality, and it is noteworthy that it is from 1990 that significant changes in social-class differentials emerge in entrants to higher education.

If sociologists of education are correct, then it pays dividends in terms of reducing inequality in attainment to delay setting and streaming within schools as long as possible. This is because, whatever the rhetoric, the logic of setting or streaming results in a different curriculum for the different sets or streams. If this were not so, there would be no need to set or stream.

The different curriculum means a less academically rich curriculum for some, and this, combined with the well-known effects of labelling children as less able in terms of low teacher expectations of their achievement, will depress rather than raise standards. The seductive efficiency of setting or streaming ignores both the fallibility of attainment measures and the fact that education is a deeply social affair, with relationships and expectations of all concerned deeply associated with attainment.

175

This fallibility indeed formed part of the case for comprehensives in the 1950s.

Two final aspects of school organisation worth considering are the changing roles and relationships among teaching staff and between teachers and parents. We are beginning to see some evidence of the changing role of the headteacher, to include financial and staffing responsibilities as well as the more traditional role of curriculum leadership. This, together with pay differentials increasing between headteachers and senior management staff on the one hand and principal teachers on the other, suggests a more clearly stratified workforce in secondary schools. This is likely to continue, especially in the context of the accountability of teachers for pupils' examination performance. The measures of school and subject departmental effectiveness mentioned in Chapters 4 and 8 emphasise the line-management relationship among senior staff, principal teachers and more junior staff. Schools, in other words, could become more hierarchical and stratified organisations unless headteachers set out deliberately to avoid this.

As far as parent–teacher relationships are concerned, the formal mechanism of school boards has not resulted in the intended greater involvement of parents in school decision-making. Chapter 9 reports the high level of parental trust in headteachers' professional expertise. The important role which parents have in the education of their children is gradually being recognised, however, and there have been several imaginative attempts to involve parents in schools, ranging from classroom helper schemes to community involvement in anti-bullying campaigns. Schools have also been opening their doors to adults wishing to return to study, and adults studying alongside young people in daytime classes is no longer an unusual sight. Will the future see schools more and more as focal points of their local communities, opening their ideas for future developments to consultation and debate? Many schools already make their accommodation, leisure facilities and learning resources available to the local community. Perhaps the changing structure of local government and the budgetary constraints under which it operates will encourage more collaboration between schools, leisure and recreation, community education and social-work services.

POLICY-MAKING

Chapters 4, 9 and 11 have highlighted the existence of the education policy community in Scotland, the relative autonomy with which it operates and the reasons for this. What will be the future direction here? This is especially difficult to analyse given the uncertainty surrounding the future establishment of a Scottish Parliament. If a Scottish Parliament is to be established, it is by no means clear how policy-making will be affected. Paterson (1996) identifies two potentially opposing effects. One scenario is that a Parliament would renew civic activism. The argument here is that there is a democratic deficit in the traditional policy process by which the Scottish Office consults with its favoured partners in Scottish civil society via quangos and other consultative mechanisms and that there is a lack of transparency in this policy process. Hence a Scottish Parliament would broaden consultation arrangements in response to a new active citizenry.

A rather different scenario is that a Parliament would lead to the strengthening of the central Scottish state, even possibly at the expense of local civic bodies. This is because there would be no guarantee that the Scottish Parliament would necessarily reflect the same political ideology as that in Westminster, and, so Paterson argues, it could encourage a strengthening of central political institutions in Scotland, so that they could reflect the Scottish majority. For education this would mean sustaining central control of the curriculum and assessment and a strengthened HMI to monitor standards. A reinvigorated civil society outcome would mean increasing local variation in the curriculum, more power being delegated to schools, and schools becoming one of the focal points of local communities (see above) with more active parent and other 'lay' participation in decision-making.

Whichever scenario unfolds, the Scottish education policy community will continue to exist, although its members may change. Two striking changes in membership are the increased prominence given to parents' groups and the decreasing role of local authorities. The reorganisation of local government into thirty-two single-tier units from the former twelve Regional and Island authorities previously governing local education has reduced their clout. There is no longer the massive Strathclyde Region, almost half of Scotland, which could exert a substantial influence on policy by reason of its size alone. In addition, devolved school management removes a good deal of financial power from local authorities, while leaving them an overall strategic and enabling role in terms of planning and provision of school places. An undoubted challenge is the reduction of places via school closures so that provision more accurately matches numbers of school pupils. Raab (1993) argues that local authorities are 'down but not out' as key players in the policy community and suggests that they still have an important influence on policy even if their influence on national education policy goals may be waning. This is likely to continue to be the picture in the future. Their position even here would be dramatically eroded if large numbers of schools sought self-governing (grant-maintained) status. This looks an unlikely, although not impossible, scenario given the balance of political opinion in Scotland. Much depends on the overall funding of local government and on the financial incentives offered to schools to become self-governing. The current financial situation of local government might pave the way for a small number of prestigious comprehensives to cut their losses and seek self-governing status. This would no doubt then encourage others.

CONCLUSION

The future directions of Scottish education are difficult to determine, although there are some things which we can predict with a fair degree of certainty. Thus, pre-fives provision will increase and the pre-fives curriculum is likely to become more uniform as nursery schools and pre-fives centres have to conform to quality standards. There will be a renewed emphasis on Scottish culture in the school curriculum. The Scottish Consultative Council on the Curriculum, as already mentioned, has already reviewed the Scottish history curriculum and is now undertaking a large consultation exercise on the more general issue of the place of Scottish culture, broadly defined, in the curriculum. There will be a tendency for more children identified as having special educational needs to be educated in mainstream settings or in units attached to mainstream.

The difficulties lie in analysing the future of curriculum provision and school organisation. Two alternatives present themselves. One is an increasingly differentiated and stratified curriculum, with children being set or streamed at age 11 or 12 in terms of 5–14 levels and continuing in a lock-step way to age 18 progressing through Standard Grade and the allocated Higher Still level, having been allocated their educational chances at an early age. The other is that the transformative potential of Higher Still will be realised, curriculum differentiation will be developed through multi-level teaching, and educational choices and chances will remain open and flexible. It is hard to remove educational opportunity from a population which has become accustomed to it. Let us hope that no political party in Scotland wants to try. It would be short-sighted not only in terms of economic performance but also in terms of the educated public which has been a cherished goal of Scottish education.

ACKNOWLEDGEMENT

My thanks to Lindsay Paterson for his comments on an earlier draft of this chapter.

REFERENCES

Barton, D. (1995) *Literacy: An Introduction to the Ecology of Written Language*, Oxford: Blackwell.

European Union (1997) *Education, Information Technology, Communications Technology and Teacher Training for the Future*, Draft Memorandum from the Presidency concerning the Informal EU Education Council, 2–3 March.

Fraser, H. (1997) *A Review of Early Intervention Programmes*, Report to SOEID, Edinburgh: SOEID.

Gamoran, A. (1996) 'Curriculum change as a reform strategy: lessons from the United States and Scotland', Paper presented at the conference on Governance and Reform, New York City, 21 August.

Gardner, H. (1993) *Multiple Intelligences: The Theory in Practice*, London: HarperCollins.

Goleman, D. (1996) *Emotional Intelligence*, London: Bloomsbury.

Halsey, A. H. (1991) 'An international comparison of access to higher education', *Studies in Comparative Education*, 1(1).

Healy, J. (1990) *Endangered Minds*, USA: New York, Simon Shuster.

HMI (1996) *Achievement for All*, Edinburgh: SOEID.

Jensen, E. (1994) *The Learning Brain*, San Diego, California: Turning Point.

McPherson, A. and Raab, C. D. (1988) *Governing Education: A Sociology of Policy since 1945*, Edinburgh: Edinburgh University Press.

Paterson, L. (1996) 'Scottish autonomy and the future of the welfare state', Paper presented at a seminar in the Department of Social Policy, Edinburgh University, 22 November.

—— (1997) 'Trends in higher education participation in Scotland', *Higher Education Quarterly* 51(1): 29–48.

Raab, C. D. (1993) 'Parents and schools: what role for education authorities?', in P. Munn (ed.) *Parents and Schools: Customers, Managers or Partners?*, London: Routledge.

SCCC (1996) *The Kist: Teacher's Handbook*, Glasgow: Nelson Blackie.

Scottish Office (1994) *Higher Still: Opportunity for All*, Edinburgh: HMSO.

Tett, L. (1997) 'Excluded voices: class, culture and family literacy', Paper presented at Exclusion and Choice Seminar, 13–15 February, Napier University.

USEFUL ADDRESSES

General Teaching Council for Scotland (GTC)
5 Royal Terrace
Edinburgh
EH7 5AF

Scottish Consultative Council on the Curriculum (SCCC)
Gardyne Road
Broughty Ferry
Dundee
DD5 1NY

The Scottish Council for Research in Education (SCRE)
15 St John Street
Edinburgh
EG8 8JR

The Scottish Office Education and Industry Department (SOEID)
Victoria Quay
Edinburgh
EH6 6QQ
(HM Inspectors of Schools Audit Unit at above address)

Scottish Qualifications Authority (SQA)
Ironmills Road
Dalkeith
Midlothian
EH22 1LE

The Scottish Schools Ethos Network (SSEN)
Moray House Institute of Education
Edinburgh
EH8 8AQ

A useful list of Scottish Education Acts is to be found in:

Homes, H. (1996) *300 Years of Scottish Education: A Handlist of the Education Acts in Scotland, 1696 to 1996,* Edinburgh: European Ethnological Research Centre.

INDEX

accountability of schools 17, 38, 56, 65, 113, 125–6, 131, 135, 151, 176
age of admission 5, 19, 36
assessment of achievement 8–10, 14–15, 36–41, 46, 57–61, 89, 95, 116–17, 123; see also Assessment of Achievement Programme, diagnostic assessment and teacher assessment
Assessment of Achievement Programme 14–15, 44–5, 116, 119–20
assisted places 5, 136
Association of Directors of Education 100, 142, 149
Audit Unit 14, 94, 116, 120, 122 see also HMI
autonomy 2, 56, 126, 138–40, 144, 146–9, 177

Bachelor of Education (BEd) 13, 106–7, 109–10, 113
baseline assessment 44
bilingualism 48–9, 81, 95, 161

Certificate of Sixth Year Studies 10, 71, 75
childminders 19–20, 22, 24
children's rights 20, 23–4
class size 36, 64, 88
Commission on Scottish Education 16–17, 45

common course 57
comprehensive education 10, 52–3, 57, 59, 62–3, 67, 78, 94, 126, 143, 145, 147, 173–4, 178
co-ordination of services 8, 19–23
curriculum 8–11, 26–32, 70, 73–5, 82, 88–90, 119, 156–169, 170–3; balance of 9–10, 35–41, 46, 164–5; continuity of 9–10, 26–7, 30–1, 35–41, 46–53, 56; see also National Curriculum Guidelines (5–14)

day centres 19, 22
devolved budgets 15, 64, 128–9
devolved school management 12, 15, 125–136, 178
diagnostic assessment 9, 42–3
disadvantage 2, 8, 28, 53, 61–2, 95, 172, 175
discipline 60, 95, 100, 102, 122, 130, 132
Dunning Report 10, 60–1

early intervention 2, 30, 87, 172
early years services 7–8, 19–25, 27–8, 32–3, 83
Educational Institute of Scotland (EIS) 98–9, 142, 149
educational psychologists 91–2
English language 9, 15, 39, 41–2, 44–6, 48, 56, 60, 71, 107, 116, 118–20, 160–2, 165, 172, 174

environmental studies 38–9, 46, 174
ethnic minorities 7, 28
ethos 14, 53, 55, 63, 94, 115, 118–19, 121–3, 132, 141
expressive arts 38–9, 46

further education 17, 68, 73, 90, 101, 106

Gaelic 7, 38, 47–8, 151, 159–61
General Teaching Council for Scotland (GTC) 12–13, 36, 52, 64, 98–105, 111, 146
governing bodies 15, 128–30, 148; see also school boards
grammar schools 59, 173–4
grant-aided schools 5–6, 85, 87
grant-maintained schools 6, 178; see also self-governing schools
guidance 52, 63, 119, 123

headteachers 15, 40, 46, 57, 63–4, 102–3, 127–135, 173, 176
Her Majesty's Inspectorate (HMI) 3, 14, 26, 37–42, 49–50, 52, 54–5, 58, 63, 65, 75–6, 84, 94–6, 110, 115, 118–20, 134, 145, 164, 172, 175, 177
Highers 10–11, 53, 70–4, 77, 107, 117, 119, 122–3
Higher Still 11, 61, 65, 67–8, 73–9, 90, 134, 146, 170–1
history 56, 60, 162–3, 165, 172, 178
homework 118
Howie Report 11, 62, 68, 72–3, 77–8, 164–5, 171

independent schools 5–6, 85, 87
individualised learning 58, 85, 92
initial teacher education see teacher education
in-service education see teacher education
inspection see Her Majesty's Inspectorate and Audit Unit

language arts 38
league tables 9–10, 42–4, 54–5, 65,
literacy 4, 27, 30, 44–5, 172
local authorities 3–4, 16, 20, 22–4, 26–7, 52–3, 57, 60, 82, 85, 93–4, 102, 117, 125, 128–31, 167, 178; reform of 4, 23–4, 94, 121, 147, 176–7

mathematics 9, 15, 38–9, 41–2, 44–6, 56–58, 60, 71, 107, 116–20, 165, 172
modern languages 38, 48–9, 56, 61
moral and religious education 38–9, 46, 56, 61
Munn Report 10, 60, 164

National Certificate 70–2, 75, 77, 90, 92, 117
National Commission on Education 16
National Curriculum 9, 38, 43–5; see also National Guidelines (5–14)
National Guidelines (5–14) 9–10, 26–7, 30–2, 35–40, 42, 45–6, 53–7, 89–90, 122, 171
national testing 9–10, 17, 41–5, 47, 57, 116–17, 149
nursery education 5, 7–8, 22, 89, 178; see also early years services
nursery vouchers 8, 24–6, 28–9

OFSTED 15, 49, 64, 115; see also HMI
omnibus schools 62, 173
opting out 52, 62, 131

parents: choice by 15, 25, 55, 62, 86, 127, 130, 132, 135, 149; communication with 10, 41–2, 89, 95–6, 127, 134; involvement of 5, 15, 31–2, 42, 81–2, 84, 100, 116, 122, 125, 127–32, 134, 149, 167, 172, 176–7

partnership, in teacher education 100–1, 108, 111–12, 173
performance indicators 14, 27, 63, 117, 123, 135
performance tables 116, 132, 135
personal and social development 39, 56
playgroups 19–21, 31
Postgraduate Certificate of Education (PGCE) 13, 103–4, 106–7, 109–11
poverty 2, 8, 21
probation, for teachers 13, 99, 101–3
professional development of teachers *see* teacher education
programme, 5–14 *see* National Guidelines (5–14)

qualifications, of teachers *see* teacher education
quality 14–15, 27, 49–50, 63, 110; assurance 8, 20, 50, 94–6, 113, 115–18

record keeping 9, 31; *see also* assessment of achievement, diagnostic assessment and teacher assessment
Record of Needs 12, 83–4, 87
registration, of teachers 13, 36, 99–104, 108
religious education 38–9, 46, 56, 61
rural schools/education 3, 6–7, 21–2, 28, 37, 47, 82

school boards 3, 5, 15, 127–136, 148–9, 151, 176; *see also* governing bodies
school development plans 14, 63, 115
school effectiveness 55, 62–4, 117, 121, 123
science 9, 15, 39, 42, 56, 61, 116–20, 172–3
Scottish Consultative Council on the Curriculum (SCCC) 9, 40, 50, 52–3, 58, 89, 134, 143, 164, 172, 178
Scottish Council for Research in Education (SCRE) 16, 42–3, 46–7
Scottish Examination Board (SEB) 9–11, 41, 52, 76, 117, 142–5
Scottish Office 3–4, 14–16, 20, 27, 35–9, 41–2, 46–8, 54–6, 62, 72–3, 82, 85, 93, 100, 104–5, 108, 117, 121, 142–8, 151–2, 177
Scottish Parliament 2, 136, 139, 150, 152–3, 173, 177
Scottish Qualifications Authority (SQA) 11, 76
Scottish Vocational Education Council (SCOTVEC) 10–11, 53, 76, 92, 143, 148
selection 10, 62, 126, 135, 143, 174–5; *see also* setting
self-governing schools 5, 36, 178
setting 10, 54, 62, 65, 95, 126, 175, 178
special educational needs 4, 40, 178; assessment of 12, 42; definition of 82–3; integration of children with 12, 52, 83–7; provision for 12, 81–9, 116
special units 12, 82, 85, 87
Standard Grade 10–11, 53–4, 56–62, 69–74, 90, 107, 117, 119, 122–3, 148, 171–3, 179
standards 10, 14–15, 49–50, 53, 56, 59, 104, 115–20; *see also* quality assurance
staying on rates 10, 53, 68–9, 174
study support 61
subject choice 60–1, 71, 74, 119

teacher assessment 9, 40–5, 116
teacher education 12–13; initial/pre-service 13, 92, 103, 105–12, 173; in-service/continuing 13–14, 58, 92–4, 112–13, 121, 173

teachers' contract 36, 64
Technical and Vocational Initiative (TVEI) 54, 90, 147–8
transition, pre-school/primary 31, 47; primary/secondary 38–9, 47, 49, 55–7

vocational education 67, 70, 73–8, 147–8, 164–7, 170

Warnock Report 82, 90